Walks in Mysterious Wiltshire

Laurence Main

Copyright © Laurence Main, 1998

Published by Sigma Leisure – an imprint of
Sigma Press, 1 South Oak Lane, Wilmslow, Cheshire SK9 6AR, England.

British Library Cataloguing in Publication Data
A CIP record for this book is available from the British Library.

ISBN: 1-85058-617-9

Typesetting and Design by: Sigma Press, Wilmslow, Cheshire.

Cover photograph: The Hag Stone (Avebury) – Laurence Main
Maps: Alan Bradley
Printed by: MFP Design and Print

Disclaimer: the information in this book is given in good faith and is believed to be correct at the time of publication. No responsibility is accepted by either the author or publisher for errors or omissions, or for any loss or injury howsoever caused. Only you can judge your own fitness, competence and experience.

PREFACE

This is a book of walks in Wiltshire, averaging five miles in length, from and to places which represent the great store of legend, magic, mystery and sense of belonging to the living land that can still be perceived by the rambler. It has two aims. One is to open the eyes of the walker to the nature of the land he or she sets foot on, so that mutual love can be exchanged and humankind can shake itself awake to the need to live in harmony with Mother Earth. The other is to invite those armchair followers of the New Age fashion and even those most worthy souls who tend their organic or veganic gardens to embrace a little bit more of the planet, to let their soft feet inform remote areas that they are not neglected and to allow places where the spirit has survived more strongly to work through us. None of these walks exceeds nine miles in length, yet the downs of Wiltshire offer enough of a challenge to stimulate the adventurous. There is a wealth of wonderful scenery and the contrast with the noisy corridors containing the motorists is made clear. The motorcar is one of the chief enemies of the living earth and it makes a nonsense of your reverence for nature if you add to the pollution and demand for more roads. The local bus or train will be glad of your support. Details of public transport are given for each walk. Tickets such as the Wiltshire Day Rover help the rambler to do without a motorcar.

Having gained confidence by following routes from a book, go out and explore Wiltshire on your own with the aid of those more precious keys to enjoying the countryside, the Ordnance Survey maps. The valuable 1:25 000 scale (2½ inch to one mile) Pathfinder maps are being replaced with Explorers.

Laurence Main

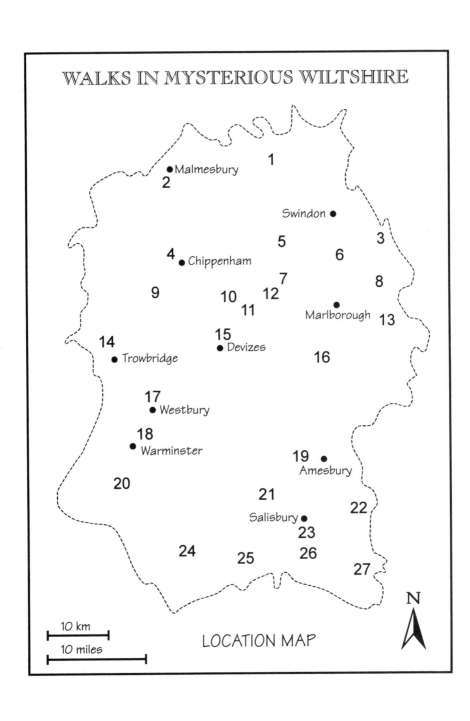

WALKS IN MYSTERIOUS WILTSHIRE

● Malmesbury
1
2

Swindon ●

5
3

● Chippenham
4
6

7
8

9
10
12

11

Marlborough
13

15
14
Devizes

● Trowbridge
16

17
● Westbury

18
● Warminster

19 ●
Amesbury

20

21
22

Salisbury ●

23

24
25
26

27

10 km
10 miles

N

LOCATION MAP

CONTENTS

INTRODUCTION

The River Wylye gave Wiltshire its name. It rises near the Deverills in the south-west corner of the county. Like may other names in Wiltshire, particularly of the rivers (most obviously the Avons), Deverill is derived from the Celtic or ancient Brythonic Welsh 'Dwfr Iâl', meaning a stream running through a fertile upland region. So, too, is Wylye, referring to the wild, raw spirit of this land, as in Myrddin Wyllt (Merlin the Wild).

Travellers coming from London perceive Wiltshire to be the first sign of untamed, magical, territory through which they speed on their way to the delights of Cornwall and Devon. The discerning pedestrian tourist knows to halt and tarry, for Wiltshire is much more than a gateway to the West Country. It is a paradise for the rambler, especially those inclined towards the mysteries posed by the remains left by our prehistoric ancestors. Tramp the downland tracks and your spirit seems to be incorporated within a vast memory of other feet, rising and falling in a rhythm that transcends millennia.

'Through the mist the light glides away. Nearer comes the formless shadow, and the visible earth grows smaller. The path has faded, and there is no means on the open downs of knowing whether the direction pursued is right or wrong, till a boulder which is a landmark is perceived.' (Richard Jefferies, *Open Air.*) Landmarks for ancient tracks tend to fall in straight lines, now recognised as leys or spirit paths (you can learn more about leys by subscribing to The Ley Hunter, PO Box 258, Cheltenham, GL35 0HR) Prehistoric landmarks don't come much bigger or of greater significance than the stones at Avebury or Stonehenge, while the pregnant belly of the goddess at Silbury Hill is the largest artificial mound in Europe. These sites are of international importance, set to dazzle pilgrims used to plainer fare. They defy our cosy perception of a barbarian past and conjure up images of a time when the gods and goddesses themselves walked this land. These stones stand so mute to unreceptive modern ears, yet could sing such rich songs to the initiated. They are like the

Moonrakers, happy to act dumb when confronted with unsympathetic officialdom but secretly laughing at our ignorance. Even so, they would reach out and speak to us if we would but acknowledge and listen to them. There is an intensity of spirit here which seeks release through channels willing to accept it. Become a walker, a living part of the landscape, and you too can enter this conspiracy. Every trip into the countryside can then become an escape from the madness of that state of encumbrance which others call civilisation.

Mother Earth is loving and kind and will reward those who draw closer to her. It is her symbol, honouring the horse-goddess Epona or Rhiannon, which is carved on so many Wiltshire hillsides – Pewsey, Alton Barnes, Westbury, Cherhill, Hackpen Hill, Broad Town, Marlborough – and who knows how many more sites? Perhaps the goddess and her helping hands are trying to attract modern minds through the crop circles which have distinguished the Wiltshire countryside in July and August in the final decades of the 20th century. Even if it is found that (most) of these are the work of human agents, could they not be working out some divine will? As King Al-

Laurence Main (left) in a crop circle below Cley Hill, near Warminster

fred the Great, who fought his most vital battle on Wiltshire soil, observed: 'There is nothing in that which men say, to wit, that a thing happens by chance.'

Alfred may not have been the first to achieve victory here. King Arthur's Badon may be the modern village of Baydon, while there must be a reason for St George's name being linked to Ogbourne. The martial spirit is strong in Wiltshire, as the Fovant Badges testify. So, too, is that altruistic concern for others which led Maud Heath's Causeway to be constructed. Wiltshire women can be formidable when defending the right, as the Earl of Pembroke discovered in the case of Grovely Wood. Neither can there be a better story of a father's love for his daughter than at Odstock, where Joshua Scamp lies buried.

The Ramblers' Association

Each walk in this book follows rights of way to which you, as a member of the public, have unrestricted access. Should you come across any problems, send full details (including grid references) to: The Ramblers' Association, 1/5 Wandsworth Road, London, SW8 2XX, telephone 0171 582 6878. Better still, join the Ramblers, go out on their group walks and volunteer to help deal with path problems yourself.

The Country Code

✔ Guard against all risk of fire.

✔ Fasten all gates. (N.B. This is the official advice. In practice, farmers usually leave gates open on purpose, so that sheep can reach water etc., so leave gates as you find them.)

✔ Keep dogs under proper control.

✔ Avoid damaging fences, hedges and walls.

✔ Keep to paths across farmland.

✔ Leave no litter.

✔ Safeguard water supplies.

✔ Protect wildlife, wild plants and trees.

✔ Go carefully on country roads.

✔ Respect the life of the countryside.

1. CRICKLADE

Route: Cricklade – Farfield Farm – Purton Stoke – Salts Hole – Cricklade

Distance: 8 miles. Easy.

Maps: OS Pathfinder 1134 Cricklade, OS Landranger 163 Cheltenham and Cirencester.

Start: The Clock, Cricklade (SU101936).

Access: Buses to Cricklade include numbers 50, 51, 52 and 53 from Swindon. (Tel. 0345 090899 for details.)

Salts Hole

Cricklade was a place of some importance in the past, being the ancient upper limit of navigation on the Thames or Isis. The museum houses silver pennies minted here in Saxon times, while the church was founded by St Sampson, or Samson, the nephew of King Arthur (being the elder son of Anna of Gwent, elder sister to Arthur and wife of Amwn Ddu), who became Bishop of Dôl in Brittany in the sixth century. His bones, or a few of them, are reputedly under the altar. Samson may have travelled here along the Roman Ermin Street, which connected Cirencester with Silchester. The clock outside the Vale Hotel brings us up to the Jubilee of Queen Victoria, which it commemorates.

The Bell Inn at Purton Stoke is the venue for the charitable distribution of rental income from pasture land which was set aside to provide revenue to compensate the poor of this parish for the loss of their common rights within the old Forest of Braydon. This land was leased to the highest bidder at a bellows auction in the Bell Inn. Instead of shouting bids, these were written down with the chalk on the bellows as it was passed around a circle of bidders. The bellows had to complete three full rounds without a new bid before the highest bidder was successful. This procedure has now been replaced by

St Samson's Church, Crickdale

the invitation of tenders for the land, but the income is still given out here every first Thursday after Epiphany (6 January).

Dr Sadler was a parishioner who eventually saw the light and made money from the well of salty water which he wanted to fill in upon settling here in the 1850s. This spring was popular with the older villagers for its healing properties, and their disgust at the doctor's treatment of it soon vanished when the doctor himself became seriously ill, tried the water and became miraculously cured. He proceeded to bottle the water for the benefit of others and his bank balance, erecting the distinctive pump room as a shelter. The sulphated and bromodated saline water was particularly good for gout, rheumatism, arthritis, the scalp, stomach, legs, liver and kidneys. Fashions change and the healing liquid is now tasted only by a dedicated few.

The Walk

1. With your back to the clock, go ahead along Calcutt Street, past Prior Park Preparatory School on your right. Pass Cricklade Museum (open Wednesdays 2-4 and Saturdays 10-12) on your left. Turn right along Spital Lane and continue over a stile to take a path along the right edge of three fields. Follow the enclosed path past a fourth field on your left. Turn left over a stile just after a gate, cut across the field to a stile in the hedge ahead and maintain this direction to a footbridge, which you cross.

2. Bear left through a field to be joined by a hedge on your left. Continue over a stile in the hedge ahead (near the corner) and bear left to take a stile beside a gate, then turn right to walk with a hedge on your right. Bear right over a stile to put the hedge on your left. You soon cross another stile and should then aim for a prominent oak tree. Cross the wooden bars in the fence below the oak and turn left over more wooden bars in another fence. Bear right diagonally through the field to a stile near a farmhouse shielded by trees.

3. Cross the stile and go ahead to the farmyard, where you turn left through a gate waymarked with a blue arrow and bear left through a field to a waymarked gate in the hedge ahead. Take it and a following gate, then turn right along a bridleway with a hedge on your left and a fence on your right.

4. Take a gate ahead and turn right with the hedged, grassy track. This bears left. Meet a hedge coming from your left and take a gate in the hedge on your right. Bear diagonally right through a field to pass tall willow trees on your left and reach a stile in the hedge ahead.

5. Cross the stile and walk beside the hedge on your right. Take a gate in the corner and turn right up a broad green drove between hedges. Continue across the course of the dismantled railway (a restored section of which may be seen a couple of miles to the south at Blunsdon) and reach a road.

6. Turn left along the road. Reach a junction and turn right for the B4041 at Purton Stoke. Cross this road to take the village street ahead, passing the Bell Inn on your right.

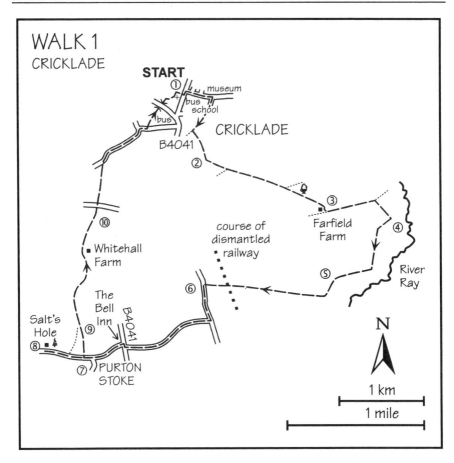

WALK 1
CRICKLADE

START

① ② museum

bus

school

bus

CRICKLADE

B4041

② ....

🔔

③

course of
dismantled
• railway

Farfield
Farm

④

River
Ray

⑤

⑩

■ Whitehall
Farm

⑥

The
Bell
Inn ⑨

B4041

Salt's
Hole

⑧ ■ 🌲

⑦ PURTON
STOKE

N

1 km

1 mile

7. Bear right with a lane at the end of the village, near a bridge. Reach an old gate which gives access to an octagonal building in a patch of woodland on your right. This is Salts Hole.

8. Retrace your steps towards Purton Stoke. Cross the bridge again and turn left over a stile. Go ahead with a hedge on your right, enter the next field and keep to its left edge. Continue over a stile and along the left edge of a third field to take another stile. Turn left over a narrow, concrete footbridge. Bear right to go through a gate in a hedge on your right.

9. Go ahead through two fields, bear very slightly left in a third and continue through a waymarked gate. Next, bear right through a gate in the hedge on your right, followed by a gate in the hedge ahead. Bear very slightly left to a gate in the next hedge. Go ahead beside a hedge on your right. Bear left with a track and walk with a hedge on your right, going ahead through a gate and passing farm buildings on your right. Continue through two sets of gates and head for the bottom right corner of a field, towards the tower of Cricklade Church.

10. Cross a stile beside a gate in the corner to follow an old green lane. Go right at a road for 30 metres, then turn left to take the signposted bridleway. Reach another road and go right to pass Upper Broadleaze Farm on your right. Pass a road called The Fiddle on your left, then soon turn left along Church Walk, taking a subway to reach St Sampson's Church. Continue to the High Street and go left to return to the clock.

2. MALMESBURY ABBEY

Route: Tourist Information Centre, Malmesbury – Abbey – Wynyard Mill – Daniel's Well – Tourist Information Centre, Malmesbury

Distance: 1¾ miles. Strenuous climb near the end.

Maps: OS Pathfinder 1152 Malmesbury, OS Landranger 173 Swindon and Devizes.

Start: Tourist Information Centre, Malmesbury (ST934872).

Access: Buses to Malmesbury include the number 31 from Swindon and Yate. (Tel. 0345 090899 for details.)

Malmesbury Abbey

John Betjeman, in one of his films, referred to medieval pilgrims

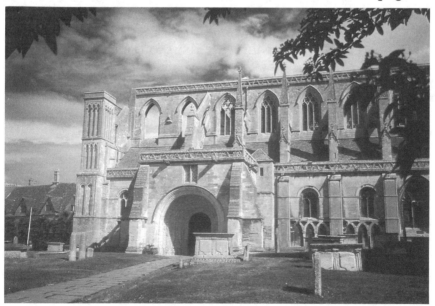

Malmesbury Abbey

feeling that they had climbed to the doors of heaven as they approached the great south porch of Malmesbury Abbey. Before 1480 they would have been guided by the abbey's magnificent spire. That fell down one night, just as Elmer, a monk who fancied himself as a pioneer aviator around 1005, crashed to the earth when he tried to fly from the top of the abbey tower. His wings and a favourable wind helped him to progress about 200 metres before he broke his legs in the fall.

The place name is probably a verbal combination of Maildulf and Aldhelm's town. Maildulf, a Scot, had founded a school and a church here by the seventh century, when St Aldhelm (639-709) became his pupil, successor and Abbot of Malmesbury. Renowned as a scholar and a magician, Aldhelm was credited with a magical flight to Rome to visit the Pope and his grave was to attract countless pilgrims. William of Malmesbury worked in the library here and wrote his 19-volume history of the kings of England before his death in 1143. King Athelstan is buried here. A grandson of Alfred, Athelstan reigned from 924 to 940 and was the first Saxon king to be acknowledged as King of England. He possessed the Spear of Longinus, or Spear of Destiny, with which the side of Jesus had been pierced at the crucifixion. Athelstan gave the spear as a wedding present to Otto the Great and it is now in the Hofburg Museum, Vienna. Malmesbury can claim to be the oldest borough in England, with the original charter dating from 924 in the reign of King Edward the Elder. King Athelstan gave the common at Malmesbury to the descendants of the men who helped him in his battles. Now known as the 'Old Corporation', they still meet regularly.

The Walk

1. Go right to Oxford Street and turn left along this to reach the Market Cross, behind which is the Abbey. Take a lane on your right to pass Abbeyfield House on your right. Continue along a narrow path signposted for the Cloistered Garden (on your left). Descend steps and bear left down more steps. Turn right at their foot to cross a bridge over the Tetbury Branch of the River Avon. Go right with a woodland path.

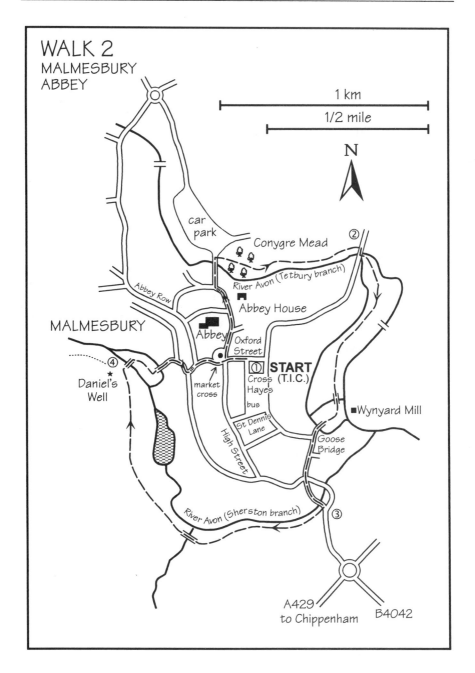

WALK 2
MALMESBURY
ABBEY

1 km

1/2 mile

N

car
park

Conygre Mead   ②

River Avon (Tetbury branch)

Abbey Row

Abbey House

MALMESBURY

Abbey

Oxford
Street

START
(T.I.C.)

④   market   Cross
Daniel's   cross   Hayes
Well   bus

■Wynyard Mill

St Dennis
Lane

High Street

Goose
Bridge

River Avon (Sherston branch)   ③

A429
to Chippenham   B4042

2. Turn right over a bridge and go left to walk downstream with the river now on your left. Bear right through a meadow with another branch of the river on your right. Pass under a former railway bridge, cross a stile beside a gate and bear left to cross a footbridge and reach Wynyard Mill. Go right at Baskerville to pass a bowling green on your right. Cross Goose Bridge and continue up St John Street. Turn left just 10 metres before turning right to cross the road and taking iron gates to a path leading to a footbridge on your left.

3. Go right with the river on your right. Walk through water-meadows, taking kissing-gates, a boardwalk and footbridges, and keeping a hedge on your right. Look for Daniel's Well on your left just after passing the end of a wall on your left.

4. Turn right across a flat, stone footbridge. Go right, then turn left over another bridge and follow the path to a junction. Turn right with a path which climbs (Burnivale). Go up steps on your left to emerge at the corner of a street. Go right to the Market Cross, Oxford Street and the Tourist Information Centre.

3. BAYDON

Route: Baydon – Pig's Hill – Membury – Hodd's Hill – Baydon

Distance: 7 miles. Moderate.

Maps: OS Pathfinder 1170 Lambourne and Aldbourne, OS Landranger 174 Newbury and Wantage.

Start: Bus stop, Baydon (SU280779).

Access: Bus number 48 runs to Baydon from Swindon and Marlborough. (Tel. 0345 090899 for details.)

The Battle of Badon (Mons Badonicus)

There are several possible sites for the Battle of Badon, including Bath, Liddington Castle (five miles west-north-west of Baydon) and Badbury Rings in Dorset. The hilltop village of Baydon, near the Roman Ermin Street, has as good a claim as the others and is my personal favourite. As I walked this route, I stopped to talk to a local resident in her garden and she was very knowledgeable about the battle and staunchly in favour of it having been fought here.

Badon was the twelfth and last of a series of battles fought by King Arthur, as recorded by Nennius in his *History of the Britons*:

'The twelfth battle was on Mons Badonis, where in one day nine hundred and sixty men were killed by one attack of Arthur, and no one save himself laid them low.'

Gildas wrote in the sixth century of the Saxons being defeated in a siege, following which there were fifty years of peace. The *Annales Cambriae* date the battle to 516 and state that, 'Arthur wore the cross of our Lord Jesus Christ on his shoulders for three full days and in which the British were victorious.' Arthur's chief opponent was probably Cerdic of the Gewissei, a Briton who courted Saxon and Jutish allies. Cerdic may have been related to Vortigern, who invited Hengist and Horsa to this land. The identification of Arthur's other chief opponent, Osla Gyllelfawr (Big Knife), is also interesting. Was he the son of Vortigern by Ronwen, the daughter of Hengist? Otherwise known as Octha II (with Octa I being Hengist), he would have been the King of Kent.

Baydon, or perhaps the nearby hill fort of Membury, would have been a strategically-placed hilltop if Osla Cyllelfawr and Cerdic had tried to outwit Arthur, whose base was in South Wales, Gloucestershire and Somerset, by advancing up the Kennet Valley rather than up the Thames Valley. Arthur may have been expecting the attack to come by way of the Thames and could have resorted to the hill forts alongside the Ridgeway which overlook the vulnerable Vale of White Horse. His opponents could have attempted to outflank Arthur, who stopped and defeated them at Baydon.

The Walk

1. From the bus stop near Downsmead (a no through road) and a telephone box, walk south, away from the church. Turn left along Manor Lane. Pass a stile in the hedge on your right. Pass Walronds Close on your right, then turn right down a lane and soon pass a signposted bridleway to Baydon House Farm on your right.

2. Fork left at a signposted junction with a bridleway (going right). Pass a pond on your right, approach woodland on your left and turn left at its edge to take a gate in a fence on your left. Turn right up the right-hand edge of a field past woodland on your right. Take a gate in the top right corner. Turn left to walk along the left edge of a field. Continue through a gate, past woodland on your left, across a track and up the right-hand edge of a field. Go left in the next corner and when the hedge on your right ends, turn right with a fence.

3. Turn right along a track. When this bears left, take a path into trees ahead, then along the left-hand edge of a field with a belt of trees on your left. Reach the hill fort of Membury, passing a wood

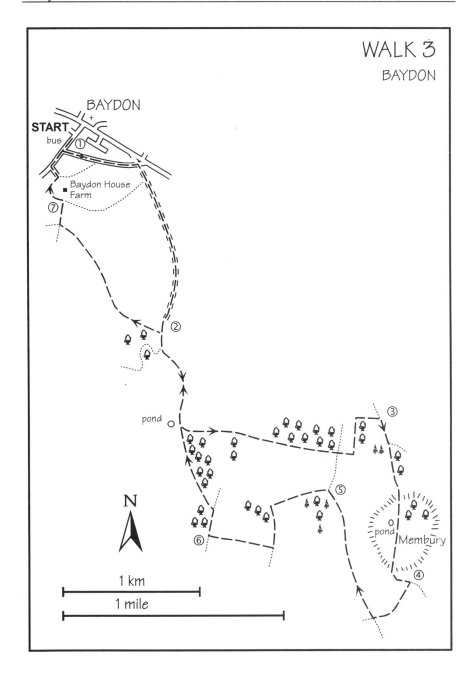

WALK 3
BAYDON

BAYDON

START
bus ①
+

Baydon House
Farm
⑦

②

pond ○

③

pond
Membury

⑤

⑥

④

N

1 km

1 mile

on your left at first. Pass a pond on your right. Leave the hill fort and bear left with a track through a gate and into a field.

4. Turn right through a gate down a track to a junction near a barn on your right. Turn right to pass the barn and continue beside a hedge on your right. Take a gate to go ahead with a fenced path.

5. Turn left at a path junction. Turn left when you come to a hedged, grassy track. Take a turning on your right.

6. Turn right at a junction, with a ruined barn at a corner on your left. Bear left at a fork to go downhill. Pass trees on your right and retrace part of your outward route to return to the signposted path junction, where you bear left (**this is actually the second turning you come to on your left,** after the site of a barn). Reach Paine's Farm and turn right at a track junction. Reach a signposted bridleway from Walrond's Farm on your right.

7. Fork left here along the signposted Alternative Bridleway to Baydon (pass Baydon House Farm on your right). Go left along the drive to a road. Turn right to walk towards the church for the bus stop near Downsmead, passing Manor Lane on your right.

4. MAUD HEATH'S CAUSEWAY

Route: Wick Hill – Kellaways – Chippenham

Distance: 5 miles in a single direction. This is a linear walk completely along roads. Take a taxi to the start and walk downhill to the finish.

Maps: OS Pathfinder 1168 Chippenham, OS Landranger 173 Swindon and Devizes.

Start: Memorial to Maud Heath at roadside on Wick Hill (ST973737).

Finish: Memorial to Maud Heath at Chippenham Clift (ST920738).

Access: Chippenham has a station on the railway between Swindon and Bath. The town can also be reached by bus (tel. 0345 090899). A taxi can be hired from Chippenham to Wick Hill. Easy's Taxis of Chippenham (tel. 01249 655471) gave me excellent service.

Maud Heath's Causeway

Ramblers may find it strange to be asked to walk completely along roads on a linear route with ends not connected by public transport (except taxis and a bus service so infrequent that even I didn't plan to use it). Maud Heath's Causeway holds a special place in Wiltshire folklore, however, so it seemed appropriate to actually walk it.

Maud Heath was a widow who walked the muddy path from Wick Hill to Chippenham market to sell her basket of eggs in the 15th century. Even today this can be an ill-drained area and Maud must have muddied her skirts many a time. In a spirit of public service, she invested her savings in land and property and provided for the construction of a causeway to benefit those who followed in her footsteps after her death.

Maid's statue, with her basket of eggs, stands on top of a column raised on Wick Hill by Henry, Marquis of Lansdowne, the Lord of the Manor, and William Bowles, the vicar of Bremhill, in 1838. There is also a stone by the roadside at this point stating:

The finish of Maud Heath's Causeway, Chippenham

'From this Wick Hill begins the praise
Of Maud Heath's gift to these highways.'

Arches carry the wayfarer above the potentially wet land at Kellaways, where another monument records the story of the causeway,
plus the injunction 'Injure me not'. The causeway's end at Chippenham is marked by another stone bearing the words:
'Hither extendeth Maud Heath's gift
For where I stand is Chippenham Clift.
Erected in 1698 but given in 1474.'

The Walk

1. Starting from the roadside monument at the top of Wick Hill, divert along the path opposite to visit the column raised in 1838
with Maud's statue at its top. Retrace your steps to the road and
go right downhill to Brembill Wick and reach a T-junction at East
Tytherton.

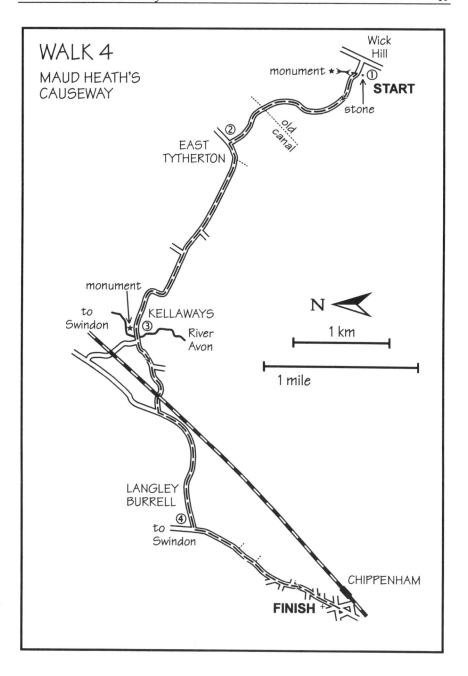

WALK 4

MAUD HEATH'S
CAUSEWAY

Wick
Hill

monument ★

① **START**

stone

old
canal

② EAST
TYTHERTON

monument

to
Swindon

KELLAWAYS
③

River
Avon

N

1 km

1 mile

LANGLEY
BURRELL

to
Swindon
④

CHIPPENHAM

FINISH

2. Fork left and pass turnings to your left, then your right.

3. Take the raised causeway, held up by arches, at Kellaways. Pass another monument and cross the bridge over the River Avon. Bear left immediately after this bridge and fork right when a road signposted for Peckingell goes left. Continue under a railway bridge and turn left to pass Langley Burrell's Brewery Arms on your left.

4. Go left at the main road and continue to the plaque marking the end of Maud Heath's Causeway opposite the church at Chippenham Clift. The railway station is nearby.

5. HACKPEN HILL

Route: Broad Hinton – The Ridgeway – White Horse – Broad Hinton

Distance: 4 miles. Easy except for one climb.

Maps: OS Pathfinder 1169 Marlborough Downs, OS Landranger 173 Swindon and Devizes.

Start: The Bell Inn, Broad Hinton (SU112765).

Access: Bus number 49 runs to Broad Hinton from Swindon and Avebury, extending to either Marlborough or Devizes, while buses numbers 5 and 6 run from Salisbury and Swindon. (Tel. 0345 090899 for details.)

Hackpen Hill White Horse

This hill figure was carved in 1838 to celebrate the previous year's coronation of Queen Victoria. It marks the spot of a far older tale, however, of a shepherd who found himself taken to the Otherworld, where he heard fairy music. He was never the same man again.

To some this is just a fairy tale, but to those who have actually slept under the stars at special times in sacred places it is easy to recognise that the shepherd was taken to Annwn, the Otherworld, where his encounters with fairies and their ways did render much of this world meaningless to him upon his return. The white horse is the symbol of the goddess Rhiannon or Epona, and Queen Victoria's coronation may have been grasped as an opportunity to restore a traditional figure which had been allowed to disappear.

Dowsing reveals a ley running at 24 degrees (28 minus 4 for magnetic variation) through the eye of the white horse. Extending this line southwards brings it through a tumulus at grid reference SU117726, to the eastern edge of Avebury's great ring (leys characteristically glance the edges of hill forts and stone circles).

Paul Devereux and Tan Thomson describe a ley running through the well and the churchyard of St Peter's, Broad Hinton, on its way to the western edge of Avebury in *The Ley Hunter's Companion*.

The Ridgeway at point 2, Hackpen Hill

The Walk

1. Face the Bell Inn and take the path going to its right, passing the pub on your left. Continue along the right-hand edges of four fields and join a track in the fifth. Take a gate ahead and climb the slope to a gate giving access to the Ridgeway.

2. Turn right along the signposted Ridgeway. Ignore a signposted byway going left. Pass a clump of trees on your right. Reach a road and cross it.

3. Turn right downhill with the signposted public footpath that goes through a kissing-gate and continues beside a fence on your left. Pass the white horse cut in the turf on your right. Descend to a road and go down it, back towards Broad Hinton.

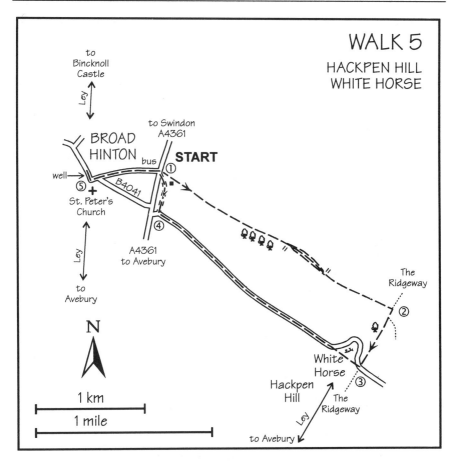

WALK 5

HACKPEN HILL
WHITE HORSE

to
Bincknoll
Castle

Ley

to Swindon
A4361

BROAD
HINTON
bus **START**
①

well→
⑤
St. Peter's
Church

B4041

④

A4361
to Avebury

Ley

to
Avebury

N

1 km

1 mile

The
Ridgeway

②

White
Horse
③
Hackpen
Hill
The
Ridgeway

Ley

to Avebury

4. Just before the main road, turn right along a no through road and emerge back at the Bell Inn and the bus stop. Extend this walk into the village to visit the church.

5. Retrace your steps through the village to the Bell Inn and the bus stop.

6. OGBOURNE ST GEORGE

Route: Ogbourne St George – The Ridgeway – Ogbourne St Andrew – Ogbourne Maizey – Dismantled Railway – Ogbourne St George

Distance: 5 miles. Easy.

Maps: OS Pathfinders 1169 Marlborough Downs and 1170 Lambourne and Aldbourne, OS Landrangers 173 Swindon and Devizes and 174 Newbury and Wantage.

Start: Bus stop near Liddiards Green, Ogbourne St George (SU199744).

Access: Buses numbers 15, 70 and 70A link Ogbourne St George with Swindon and Marlborough. (Tel. 0345 090899 for details.)

A Solar Giant

Og was the Celtic solar giant, so it is appropriate that the Christian St George should become associated with this significant point on the famous Dragon Line that runs across southern Britain and passes through Glastonbury Tor and Avebury. Read more about this in *The Sun and the Serpent* by Hamish Mil1er and Paul Broadhurst. Hamish Miller's dowsing has led him to distinguish controversial Michael (male) and Mary (female) energy currents coiled around the straight ley of the Dragon Line. These currents converge at a mound in the churchyard of Ogbourne St Andrew.

The Walk

1. With your back to the bus shelter and Liddiards Green, go right and soon pass a signposted public footpath on your right and a school on your left. Pass a signposted public footpath on your left. Cross a stream and turn right along a lane to the church. Continue past the church on your right and turn right to pass a gate on your left. Turn left over a stile in the hedge shortly after the gate. Continue over a stile in the shade of trees and through a field to reach a road signposted as the Ridgeway.

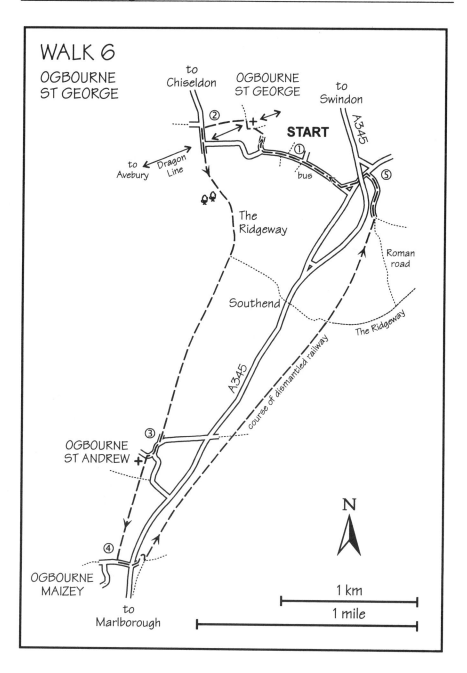

WALK 6
OGBOURNE
ST GEORGE

2. Turn left along the road to a bend where it goes left. Take the signposted Ridgeway straight ahead along a concrete byway. When the Ridgeway turns left, as signposted, go straight ahead with this signposted byway, now a grassy track.

3. Go right at a road in Ogbourne St Andrew and visit the church on your right. Passing the church on your right, take the path running south with a small housing estate on your left. Emerge over a stile to go through a field and cross another stile in a fence ahead. After the next field, reach a road at Ogbourne Maizey.

4. Go left to the A345. Cross this road carefully and take the signposted byway opposite which bears left to the course of a dismantled railway. Go left along this.

5. When you reach a road, turn left along it to Ogbourne St George. Turn left at a crossroads and pass under a flyover. Fork right and turn right to return to the bus stop near Liddiards Green.

Ogbourne St George Church

7. THE SANCTUARY

Route: West Overton – The Sanctuary – The Ridgeway – Fyfield Down – West Overton

Distance: 6 miles. Moderate. This walk can be linked with Walk 12.

Maps: OS Pathfinders 1169 Marlborough Downs and 1185 Devizes and Marlborough, OS Landranger 173 Swindon and Devizes.

Start: Bus stop at North Farm, West Overton (SU133685).

Access: Bus number 49A (Swindon-Avebury-Marlborough) serves the village of West Overton, while buses numbers 5 and 6 stop at North Farm on the A4 as they go between Salisbury and Swindon. (Tel. 0345 090899 for further details.)

The Sanctuary

Imagination is required when you visit the site of the Sanctuary today, but this used to be an impressive site, described by Samuel Pepys in 1668 as having 'great high stones pitched round – in some measure like that of Stonehenge'. His contemporary John Aubrey noted two concentric rings of sarsens. Stukeley, who recorded the use of Sanctuary as the site's name, witnessed its destruction in 1724, when the land was ploughed up and the stones removed. It wasn't until 1930 that archaeology was to show us how the Sanctuary had once been. As to why any structure was erected here, the answer may well be contained within the covers of Michael Dames's book *The Avebury Cycle*. Dames joins the antiquarian Stukeley in recognising a great serpent, or serpents, formed by Avebury's stone avenues. The Sanctuary was seen as the snake's head by Stukeley, while Dames prefers to view it as the tip of the tail. This classic symbol for the life force may have hibernated at the Sanctuary before reawakening at Imbolc (1st February), and proceeding to Avebury and Silbury, as described in Walk 12 (which can be linked with this route).

The circles of the Sanctuary's ground plan could indicate the way between worlds and could have suited circle or spiral dances. Could this have been a maze or labyrinth? A wooden hut stood in the centre of the Sanctuary, similar to structures which stood during the same Neolithic period at Woodhenge and Durrington Walls in the Stonehenge area and at the heart of Silbury Hill. There may well have been an open 'eye' at the centre of its roof to allow in the light of the moon and the sun.

The Michael and Mary currents described by Hamish Miller and Paul Broadhurst in *The Sun and the Serpent* cross at the Sanctuary. This walk takes you past the recumbent sarsen stones on Fyfield Down. They are nicknamed 'grey wethers' because they can appear like sheep.

The Walk

1. Take the road signposted for West Overton leading away from North Farm. Bear right at a fork before the church. Follow this road as it bends right.

2. Go right at a road junction. After 50 metres, bear left along a narrow path past gardens and garages. Cross a road to continue with the narrow path. Rejoin the road to maintain your direction along it, ignoring a turning on your left.

3. Reach East Kennett and turn right along a lane. Cross a bridge over the River Kennett and go left at a signposted junction. If you are linking this route to Walk 12 (Avebury), you could take a path going left. Otherwise continue this route by walking uphill with a hedge on your left to reach the Sanctuary on your left.

4. Go ahead across the A4 road and continue northwards with the signposted Ridgeway. Pass a signposted bridleway on your left.

5. Turn right at a signposted crosstracks to follow a bridleway through a gate and towards trees. Continue past sarsens in the National Nature Reserve of Fyfield Down. Take gates, cross gal-

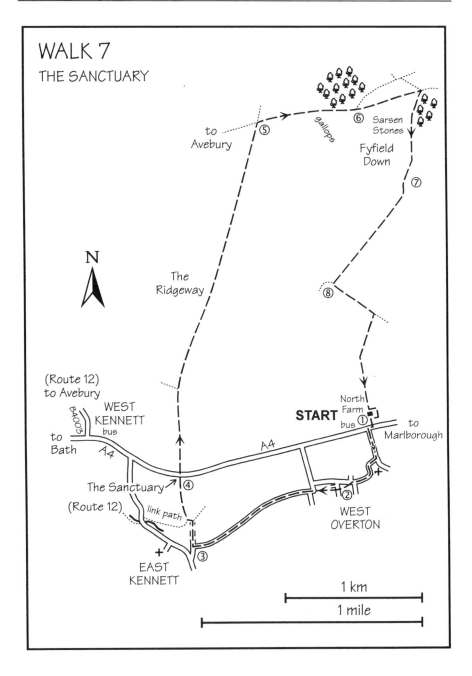

WALK 7
THE SANCTUARY

to Avebury ⑤

gallops

⑥ Sarsen Stones

Fyfield Down

⑦

N

The Ridgeway

⑧

(Route 12) to Avebury

WEST KENNETT
bus

North Farm
START bus ① to Marlborough

to Bath   A4

A4

The Sanctuary ④

(Route 12)   link path

WEST OVERTON

②

EAST KENNETT

③

1 km

1 mile

lops and descend along a firm track past a corner of woodland on your left.

6. When the track bears left, take a grassy path ahead towards more trees, passing more sarsens. Take a gate and turn right to walk with the woodland on your left. Bear right over a stile and go left beside a fence on your left and sarsens on your right. Ignore a gate on your left and keep beside the fence on your left as you go ahead.

7. Ignore a gate and stile on your left. Bear right to cut across downland to a corner of a hedge on your left. Continue beside a fence on your left and take a gate ahead, still keeping the fence on your left. Go ahead through another gate.

8. Turn left along a farm track, passing a house on your right. Take a gate ahead, pass a big shed and turn right along a firm farm track. Go left, then right, through the farmyard at North Farm to reach the A4 and the bus stop.

8. LITTLECOTE HOUSE

Route: Ramsbury – Littlecote House – Ramsbury

Distance: 6 miles. Easy

Maps: OS Pathfinder 1170 Lambourne and Aldbourne, OS Landranger 174 Newbury and Wantage.

Start: The Bell (bus stop), Ramsbury (SU276716).

Access: Buses to Ramsbury include number 48 from Swindon and Marlborough, and number 48A, which links Swindon with Hungerford. (Tel. 0345 090899 for details.)

Wild Darrell's Baby

One night in 1575, when Littlecote House was owned by the Darrell family, a midwife was taken blindfolded to a richly-furnished bedroom, where a fierce and domineering man watched a lady give birth to a son. He threw the baby on the fire before dismissing the midwife, who had secretly cut off a piece of the bed-curtain. The alert midwife also counted the stairs as she was led away blindfolded, returned to her home and paid generously in gold. She went straight away to a magistrate to unburden her conscience. A search led to Littlecote House, where the number of stairs and a missing piece of curtain clinched its identification as the scene of the murder. William Darrell, the haughty man, bribed his trial judge, Sir John Popham, to allow him to go free. However, he didn't escape divine wrath as within a short time he fell from his horse to his death. His ghost is said to mark the spot where he fell, while his sister, the baby's mother, haunts the house. A ghostly coach and horses driven by 'Wild' Darrell was seen when the heir of Littlecote died in 1831.

So goes the old tale, but its details don't bear investigation. William Darrell died in 1588, while Sir John Popham became a judge in 1591. However, letters have been found which suggest that William Darrell did murder his child by a woman in the household of Sir

Henry Knyvett of Charlton. This woman was the sister of a Mr Bonham in the household of Sir John Thynne of Longleat, where a letter dated 2nd January, 1578 (1579 in modern terms) was discovered. The other letter was a statement by a magistrate of a deathbed deposition by a midwife, Mrs Barnes of Shefford, of a strong smell of burning after attending to the birth of a baby to a lady who wore a mask at Charlton House. William Darrell did give Littlecote House to Sir John Popham.

Littlecote has a long history. A large Roman mosaic was unearthed when trees were being planted in Littlecote Park in 1727. Edward Popham, the current owner, had it covered to deter archaeologists from visiting. Detailed drawings were made of it first, however. Popham pretended that he had destroyed it and suggested that its site was a quarter of a mile from its real one. Pieces of Roman floors brought to the surface by the activity of rabbits at the time of a survey of the park in 1976 led to the rediscovery of the mosaic in 1977. It portrays Orpheus, whose cult rivalled Christianity in the fourth century. Woodchester in Gloucestershire can boast a similar mosaic. See the Orpheus Mosaic and tour Littlecote House on Sundays and Wednesdays in the summer (tel. 01488 682509).

The Walk

1. Face the Bell and go right, signposted for Hungerford. Take the pavement down to a fork and bear right, as signposted for Froxfield (Wiltshire Cycleway). Cross a bridge over the River Kennett. Pass a lane to Lamplands on your right.

2. Turn left along a firm track, signposted as a public bridleway, to Littlecote House. Pass a signposted bridleway on your right (along which you will return). The track becomes grassy after the West Lodge. Keep to the left-hand side of the field.

3. Continue, now on a metalled drive, and pass Littlecote House on your left. Walk on to the East Lodge and a road.

4. Go right up the road and when it turns left, go straight ahead

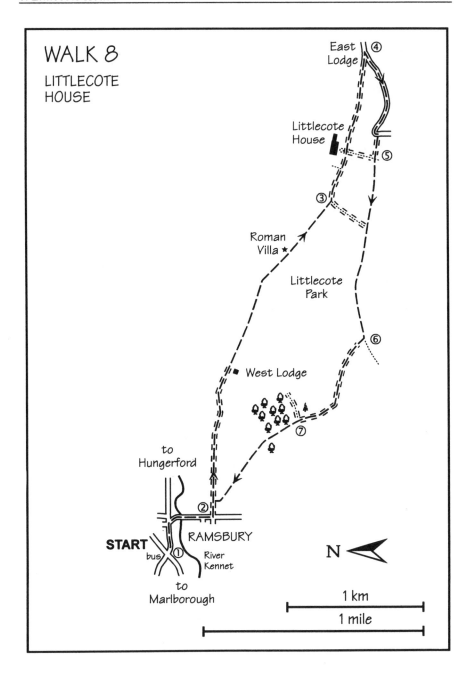

WALK 8
LITTLECOTE
HOUSE

East Lodge ④

Littlecote House

⑤

③

Roman Villa ★

Littlecote Park

⑥

West Lodge

⑦

to Hungerford

②

START
bus ①
RAMSBURY
River Kennet

to Marlborough

N

1 km

1 mile

Littlecote House

along the drive into Littlecote Park (signposted as a public foot-path to Ramsbury). When the drive turns right, go ahead along a track. When this track turns right, go ahead along a track with grass down its middle.

5. Fork right along a concrete track until the lane bends right to a 'private' sign. Fork left along a path, keeping just inside woodland.

6. Descend with a hedged path to rejoin the outward path. Go left to retrace your steps to Ramsbury.

9. LACOCK

Route: Lacock – River Avon – Lacock

Distance: 2¼ miles. Easy.

Maps: OS Pathfinder 1184 Melksham, OS Landranger 173 Swindon and Devizes.

Start: The George Inn, Lacock (ST915685).

Access: Buses to Lacock include number 234, running between Chippenham and Trowbridge. (Tel. 0345 090899 for details.)

The Home of Photography

Lacock is a special village, now in the care of the National Trust, and the location of period films such as *Pride and Prejudice*. The village can be visited free of charge at any time, but admission charges and opening times apply to both the Abbey (tel. 01249 730277) and the Fox Talbot Museum (tel. 01249 730459). William Henry Fox Talbot was a man of many talents who was born in the Abbey in 1800 and lies buried in Lacock cemetery. He is most remembered as 'the father of photography', having invented the way of obtaining prints from a negative. He took his very first photograph of the Oriel Window at the Abbey. He was also the first to decipher the Syrian and Chaldean cuneiform texts.

If Lacock is where the mystery of photography was solved, it is also where a story of forbidden romance had a happy ending. Sir Henry Sharington inherited Lacock Abbey from his brother in 1553. Olive, his daughter, fell in love with John Talbot against her father's wishes. Walking the battlements in the hope of remote contact with her lover in the bushes below, on an impulse, Olive jumped down to him. Her skirts acted like a parachute in the wind. John wasn't so lucky, being knocked out as if dead. Secrecy was now replaced by frantic cries for help. The result was that Sir Henry consented to their marriage. Olive's husband and father both died in 1581. She outlived her son and died in 1646, when her grandson, Sharington Talbot, was the master of the house. Lacock Abbey had been granted to Olive's uncle, Sir William Sharington, at the Dissolution. He became notorious for fraud when vice-treasurer of the Bristol mint. He must have covered his tracks expertly and made a fortune because he obtained a pardon and was able to buy back his estates. He served as Sheriff of Wiltshire in 1552.

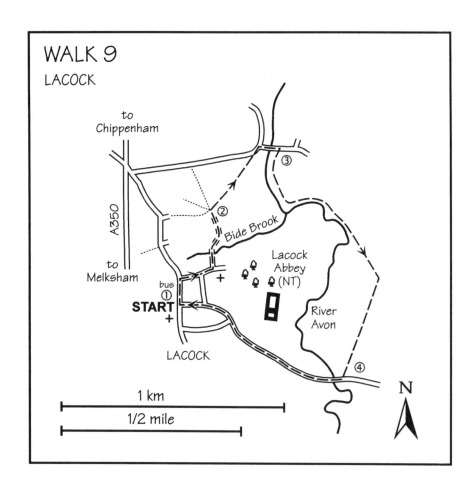

The Walk

1. With your back to the George Inn, cross the road and go left, then fork right along Church Street. Approach St Cyriac's Church and turn left up a no through road. Cross a packhorse bridge and walk downstream with Bide Brook on your right.

2. At the end of the lane, bear right through a kissing-gate and through a field to another kissing-gate. Reach a road, go right and almost immediately turn right over a bridge across the River Avon.

3. Turn right over a stile to walk downstream beside the river on your right. Continue over two stiles, cut across to a gate in a hedge ahead, then bear right through a meadow to a footbridge. Bear slightly right in the next meadow to take a stone stile beside a signpost to the left of a bridge (there is a second bridge on your left which spans what is usually dry land).

4. Turn right to cross the bridge and follow the elevated pavement back to Lacock. Fork right to pass the entrance to the museum and Abbey on your right. Continue by bearing left up the High Street (passing East Street on your right). When you reach West Street, the bus stop and the George Inn are on your right, hut divert left to see Fox Talbot's grave in the cemetery.

10. CHERHILL WHITE HORSE

Route: Cherhill – Oldbury Castle – Cherhill

Distance: 3½ miles. Strenuous.

Maps: OS Pathfinders 1169 Marlborough Downs and 1185 Devizes and Marlborough, OS Landranger 173 Swindon and Devizes.

Start: Black Horse pub, Cherhill (SU035700).

Access: Bus number 93 runs to Cherhill from Calne and Avebury. (Tel. 0345 090899 for further details.)

Of Horses and Monuments

Climb to enjoy the view from the Iron Age earthworks of Oldbury Castle and you are confronted with two fairly recent monuments which raise questions about what certain people knew about leys and sacred sites in the 18th and 19th centuries. Start and finish this walk at a pub with an interesting name.

The white horse carved above Cherhill occupies the sort of site that an ancient predecessor might well have occupied. There is no record of a white horse here before Dr Alsop of Calne bellowed instructions through a megaphone from the main road to workmen cutting it in 1780. Did the 'mad doctor' know something, or was he acting as a channel for the spirit of the place, with the white horse suggesting the goddess Rhiannon or Epona, without realising it himself?

The third Marquess of Lansdowne may have been led by masonic knowledge to build his monument in 1845 in memory of Sir William Petty, a 17th century economist. Such monuments mark leys, in my experience. Whether the marquess, like Dr Alsop, was fully aware of what he was doing is another question. Dowsing for the most important ley or spirit path at Oldbury Castle, I found that it led through the monument (from tumuli in the west at SU038694 and SU039694) along the right of way across the interior of Oldbury Cas-

Cherhill White Horse

tle to leave by its eastern exit. Extending this line eastwards through a tumulus at SU115688 leads to the Marlborough white horse at SU185681. Dowsing leys is not fashionable with some ley hunters, but this is the ley I dowsed and I had a friend with me who confirmed it. I simply asked for the primary ley. I must admit that I had wondered, even expected, this ley to run to the nearby white horse. There is, indeed, another ley which I also dowsed which does just that. The most important ley, however, pointed in another direction. Only later, when I had taken its compass bearing (94 degrees, being 98 less 4 for magnetic variation) and drawn its line on the map did I find that it led to the white horse – but at Marlborough!

So much for white horses. The pub is a reminder of the b1ack horses ridden by King Arthur's knights when they patrolled the border between Celt and Saxon in the sixth century. At least that is what S.G. Wildman's book *The Black Horsemen* proposes. Sadly, S.G. Wildman died before I could invite him to speak at the Ley Hunter's Moot in 1991. I have since met his daughter, working for CADW at Valle Crucis Abbey. S.G. Wildman was obviously a gentleman and a scholar whose book is worthy of consideration.

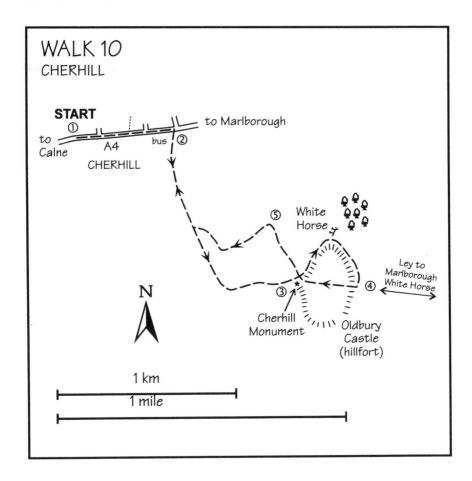

The Walk

1. Face the Black Horse pub and go right along the pavement of the A4. Pass Middle Lane (twice) and a signposted footpath on your left, then turn right to cross the road carefully and take a signposted bridleway towards the Downs. The white horse is on the hillside ahead on your left and the monument is to the right of it, with the earthworks of the hill fort between. Pass a stile on your left.

2. Bear left over a stile near the top gate and walk towards the prominent monument. Continue past the hill fort on your right to Cherhill White Horse.

3. Turn your back on the view over the vale and walk with the edge of the hill fort on your right until an entrance invites you to look through its interior to the monument (along the line of the primary ley linking it with Marlborough White Horse).

4. Turn right to follow the ley to the monument. Bear right downhill from it.

5. Turn left to walk with a fence on your right. Cross a stile to regain access to your outward track and go right down it. Cross the road with care and turn left along the pavement to retrace your steps to the Black Horse pub.

11. THE WANSDYKE

Route: Shepherd's Shore (request bus stop) — Wansdyke — Roman road — Shepherd's Shore (request bus stop)

Distance: 5 miles. Moderate.

Maps: OS Pathfinder 1185 Devizes and Marlborough, OS Landranger 173 Swindon and Devizes.

Start: Shepherd's Shore request bus stop (SU045663).

Access: Bus number 49 (Swindon to Avebury and Devizes) serves the request bus stop at Shepherd's Shore. (Tel. 0345 090899 for further details.)

The Wansdyke

The 50 miles of the Wansdyke, with its impressive banks and ditch, running from Savernake Forest in the east to Dundry Hill, south of Bristol, in the west, gives much to wonder at and to wander along, but renders little information about its origin. Attributed to Woden by the Saxons, this is most probably their salute to the scale of the thing rather than an indication that they dug it. The favourite link is with the fifth century Romano-Britons, when this may have been a tribal boundary, perhaps in the days of Ambrosius Aurelianus, a generation before King Arthur. Archaeology has shown that it cannot have existed before the very last phase of Roman rule in Britain. It was probably more of an agreed frontier than a manned barrier, its length would have extended the greatest of contemporary armies. Chris Barber in *Journey to Avalon* plumps for Ambrosius constructing it in the fifth century to defend Domnonia (modern Devon and Cornwall) from a Saxon army coming up the Thames Valley. But what about Cerdic's approach from the south in the late fifth and early sixth centuries? Truly, this mighty earthwork is a mystery.

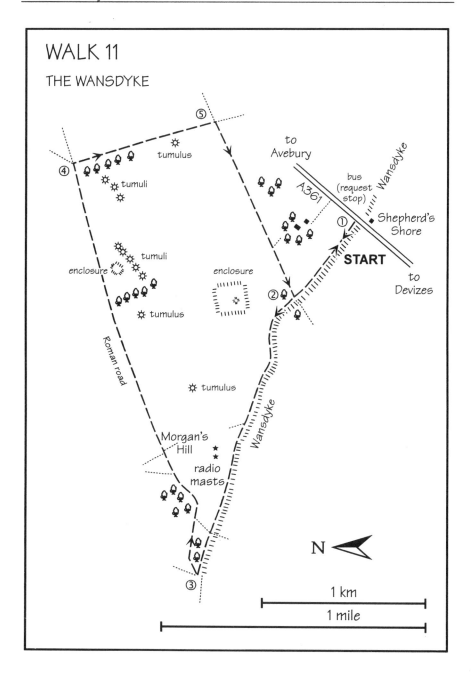

WALK 11

THE WANSDYKE

The Walk

1. Go north with the Wansdyke to a path junction.

2. Cross a track to take the path waymarked with a blue arrow which goes through a belt of trees. Emerge through a gate and go ahead with the Wansdyke. Continue through three gates, pass radio masts on Morgan's Hill on your right and ignore an inviting waymarked path through a gate on your left. Continue to a track junction.

3. Turn right along an old Roman road, passing trees on your right at first, then on your left. Continue past a belt of trees on your right and notice tumuli in the field on your right.

4. Reach a plantation of trees on your right and turn right through a gate to walk with these trees on your right.

5. Turn right with a track. Pass an access track to a farm on your left. Continue to trees on your right and turn left to retrace your steps down the Wansdyke to the request bus stop at Shepherd's Shore.

12. AVEBURY

Route: Avebury – West Kennett – Silbury Hill – Avebury

Distance: 5 miles. Easy. This walk can be linked with Walk 7.

Maps: OS Pathfinder 1185 Devizes and Marlborough, OS Landranger 173 Swindon and Devizes.

Start: Red Lion, Avebury (SU102699).

Access: Buses run to Avebury from Swindon (numbers 5, 6 and 49), Salisbury (5 and 6), Devizes (number 49) and Calne (number 93). (Tel. 0345 090899 for details.)

The Landscape Goddess

Much has been written about Avebury since John Aubrey observed in 1648 that it 'does as much exceed in greatness the so renowned Stonehenge, as a cathedral does a parish church'. Michael Dames has been inspired to write two classic books which are indispensable guides to true pilgrims. *The Silbury Treasure* asserts Silbury Hill to be the pregnant belly of the Great Goddess – a womb rather than the long-supposed tomb. Dated to the Lugnasadh (around 1st August) period of about 2660BC, in the Neolithic Age, this is the supreme Harvest Hill, linking the gathering of the summer's fruits with the goddess giving birth. Expanding on this theme, Michael Dames's second book, *The Avebury Cycle*, explores the other parts of this sacred area and the retreat, with the onset of winter at Samhain (early November), into the underworld of the Tomb Lady at West Kennett long barrow. This was constructed around 3250BC, but the forecourt 'ox' stones date from the same time as Silbury Hill.

Link this route with Walk 7 to visit the Sanctuary, thought to be linked with Imbolc (1st February) and the coming of spring. The stone avenues are seen by Dames as two snakes which entwine at Avebury, although Stukeley perceived them as forming one serpent when he came this way in the 18th century. The stones forming the

Avebury

apparently processional ways are easily seen as alternately male and female. Did dancers weave between them on their way to the great wedding ring of Avebury at Beltane (May Day)? This time before Christians, as Dames puts it, 'expelled themselves from Eden with their masochistic belief in Original Sin' was when Nature and culture lived in Harmony.

Another author with important insights to share on the Avebury complex is Paul Devereux. Read his special study of this 'landscape of the mind' in *Symbolic Landscapes*. Noting that archaeologists reckon West Kennett long barrow was extended westwards, Devereux reasons that this extension could have coincided with the raising up of Silbury Hill. It enables a sight line to appear, taking in West Kennett long barrow, Silbury Hill and Windmill Hill. More significantly, it can be seen to work on the vertical dimension. Our Neolithic ancestors didn't look at lines on maps!

Another precise sight line goes from the site of the obelisk at the centre of the southern inner circle at Avebury to the top of Silbury Hill. What's more, this sight line was harvest-dependent, being obstructed by a cereal crop on Waden Hill. These and other sight lines intersect Silbury's profile between the hill's curious ledge and its flat summit. This ledge was also found by Devereux to allow a view of a 'double sunrise' at Beltane and, crucially, at Lugnasadh.

Looking at the stones, particularly those in the West Kennett Avenue, it is easy to discern human and animal shapes – simulacra. Look for the hag stone and another resembling a horse's head. As Paul Devereux heard when on Silbury Hill, 'In this Mystery shall we dwell.'

The Walk

1. With your back to the Red Lion, cross the road carefully to take a little gate ahead on your left into one quadrant of Avebury's great stone circle. Walk south with the road on your right and leave by a small gate beyond the bank and ditch of the henge. Bear right across the road, although avoiding the road on your right.

2. Take a small gate to enter the West Kennett Avenue, with its male and female stones. Look for the horse and hag stones. There is a gate giving access to the road on your left at the end of this avenue. You can avoid walking along the road by going ahead over a stile at the bottom of the avenue and walking with the road still on your left until a stile invites you to turn left over it. Immediately turn right to follow this final stretch of the B4003 to its junction with the A4 at West Kennett.

3. Turn left beside the A4 and take a turning on your right towards East Kennett. Approach a bridge across the River Kennett. If you are linking this route with Walk 7 (The Sanctuary), turn left along a fieldpath here to join it. Continue this route by going ahead over the bridge.

4. Turn right along a track to reach a staggered path junction where you pass a path on your left, go ahead 10 metres and then turn right along a narrow path. Emerge over a stile and continue along the left-hand edge of a meadow. Take a gate in its far left corner.

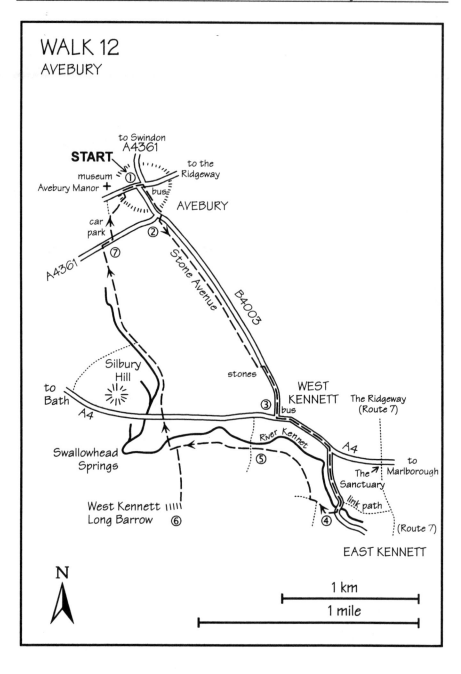

WALK 12
AVEBURY

5. Cross a lane and go ahead along a track. Silbury Hill can be seen ahead on your right. Continue over a stile beside a gate and along the foot of a field. Turn left at a path junction to divert up to West Kennett long barrow.

6. Retrace your steps to the path junction and go left to reach the A4. Cross this road, take a gate and walk along the left-hand edge of a field, with Silbury Hill across the Winterbourne on your left. Continue through a gate and beside the stream on your left. Maintain this direction over a stile and past a bridge bringing another path from your left. Go right at a road.

7. Immediately after the car park on your left, turn left along the signposted path back to the village of Avebury, where the bus stops and the Red Lion pub are in the centre, at the staggered crossroads.

13. GREAT BEDWYN

Route: Great Bedwyn – Wilton Windmill – Wilton Water – Kennet and Avon Canal – Great Bedwyn

Distance: 6 miles. Moderate.

Maps: OS Pathfinder 1186 Hungerford and Savernake Forest, OS Landranger 174 Newbury and Wantage.

Start: Great Bedwyn railway station (SU280646).

Access: Trains run to Bedwyn from Reading and London Paddington. Buses to Great Bedwyn include the number 20 from Marlborough and Hungerford. (Tel. 0345 090899 for details.)

Ben Lloyd

Exploring mysterious Wiltshire requires a visit to Great Bedwyn because of Ben Lloyd. A man who does his reading and writing through the carving of stone, he can lead you on a tour of St Mary's Church and read the stonework like a book. In his company you realise that much knowledge was held and passed on by masons in the days before almost universal literacy. By learning how to read books, it seems we have lost the simplicity of mind to read what is obvious in stonework. During the Second World War, Ben Lloyd's ability to see patterns hidden to conventional minds led to him deciphering German codes. Spend time near the end of this walk visiting Great Bedwyn's Stonemason's Museum. Enter St Mary's Church too. Ben Lloyd asserts that leys converge on it and that Bedwyn is derived from the Welsh 'Bedd Gwyn' (white grave). One grave that you can see in the church is that of Sir John Seymour (1476-1536), father of Jane Seymour, Henry VIII's third wife and mother of Edward VI. His uncle, Edward Seymour, Duke of Somerset, became Lord Protector when the nine-year old succeeded to the throne. Also buried here is William Seymour (1588-1660), great-grandson of Sir John and grandson of the Lord Protector. He secretly married Lady Arabella

Stuart, next in line to the throne when her cousin James succeeded Elizabeth I. It was treason for her to marry without the sovereign's permission so the couple were arrested. They attempted to escape to France, but Lady Arabella was caught. William went into exile alone. He returned after his love had died a prisoner in the Tower of London and led Royalist forces in the Civil War.

Wilton Windmill has been restored and is open on summer Sunday afternoons. Flour milled here is for sale then. More industrial archaeology is nearby in the shape of Crofton Beam Engines, still pumping water to the summit level of the Kennet and Avon Canal. These are open daily in the summer (tel. 01672 870300).

The Walk

1. Take the road away from Great Bedwyn, crossing the bridge over the Kennet and Avon Canal. Turn right along the towing path to walk with the canal on your right. Reach a bridge over the canal and bear left here, over a stile beside a gate, to leave the canal and walk with trees on your left. Ignore the first stile in the fence on your left. Continue to the end of the trees before turning left over a stile and bearing right to a signpost beside a stile near the far right corner of this field. Cross this stile to a road.

2. Go left along the road for 20 metres, then turn right with a grassy track beside a fence on your left. Continue past woodland on your left.

3. Turn left over a stile beside a gate into the wood. Bear left up a woodland ride, climb to a crosspaths and descend to a gate giving access to a road. Turn right along this for 100 metres.

4. When the road bends right, take the signposted grassy track going left. Bear right at a fork to pass a pond on your left. Go ahead through woodland and along a track to a road. Turn right to pass Wilton Windmill on your left.

5. Fork left, signposted for Crofton Beam Engines. Reach a junction at the edge of Wilton and turn right along the course of a Roman

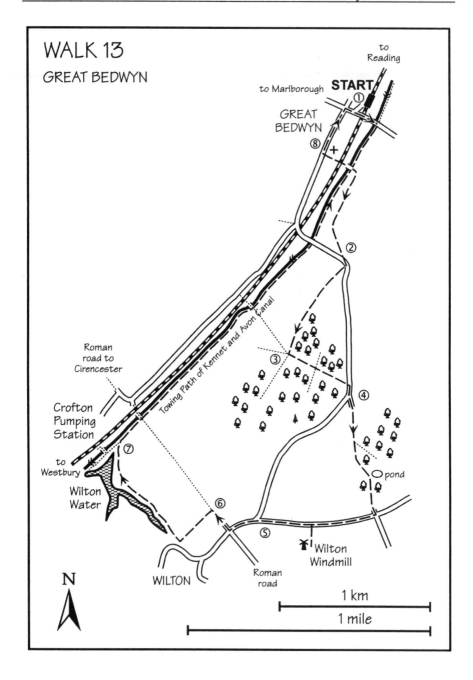

WALK 13
GREAT BEDWYN

to Reading

to Marlborough   **START**
①
GREAT
BEDWYN
⑧ ✚

②

Towing Path of Kennet and Avon Canal

Roman
road to
Cirencester

③

④

Crofton
Pumping
Station

⑦

to
Westbury

Wilton
Water

⑥

⑤

pond

Wilton
Windmill

WILTON   Roman
road

N

1 km

1 mile

road. Look out for a stile beside a signpost on your left. **(This is not the first stile at the end of the first field.)**

6. Turn left over the stile to take the signposted path through a field down towards Wilton. Just before reaching a road, turn right with the signposted path along the left-hand edge of the field. Pass Wilton Water on your left.

7. At the canal, you could divert left and across the canal to see the Crofton Pumping Station. Continue this route by going right along the towing path with the railway and canal on your left. Go ahead to lock 64 and bridge 96 (Church Lock). Turn left across this bridge, continue over the railway with care and walk with the wall of the churchyard on your right.

8. Go right along the village street, visiting St Mary's Church on your right and the Stonemason's Museum on your left. Reach the end of Church Street and turn right down Brook Street to return to the railway station.

14. BRADFORD-ON-AVON

Route: Bradford-on-Avon — Budbury — Saxon church — Tithe barn — Avoncliff Aqueduct — Kennet and Avon Canal — Bradford-on-Avon

Distance: 4½ miles. Strenuous up to Budbury, otherwise easy.

Maps: OS Pathfinders 1184 Melksham and 1200 Westbury and Trowbridge, OS Landranger 173 Swindon and Devizes.

Start: Railway station, Bradford-on-Avon (ST825607).

Access: Bradford-on-Avon has a station on the railway between Bath and Westbury. Buses include the X4 (Salisbury-Bath). (Tel 0345 484950 for National Rail Enquiries. Tel 0345 090899 for bus information.)

A Lost Ancient Settlement and a Lost Saxon Church

To lose one ancient sacred site may be unfortunate, to lose two appears to be carelessness on the part of the people of Bradford-on-Avon. At least you can see the seventh-century Saxon church, now rediscovered after having been 'lost'. The major prehistoric site at Budbury is now covered by a housing estate. Budbury Circle is now a road serving the backs of houses, not a ring of ancient standing stones.

This broad ford of the Avon has attracted human settlement from prehistory. The very name of the river indicates that the old Celtic tongue lingered on here. Guy Underwood, author of The *Pattern of the Past*, found two barrows, three mazes and Neolithic pottery at Budbury, with the whole enclosed by a double-ditch. Most interestingly, this eminent archaeologist recorded that this prehistoric site was found by dowsing.

A small part of the orchard which Guy Underwood dowsed to indicate that the site was 'appropriate to the cultivation of the sacred apple' survives at Budbury Farm. Perhaps St Mary's Church, Tory, occupies an ancient sacred site below Budbury. Why else should it be built on so high a hill? It is also on an ancient route to Glaston-

St Mary's Church, Tory

bury. A sacred spring pours forth from its foot, now known as Lady Well. Is this an echo of ancient goddess worship? Perhaps the finest example in England of a Saxon church is further down the hill. Dedicated to St Laurence, this dates from the seventh century. This church was neglected after the consecration of the parish church, dedicated to the Holy Trinity, in about 1150. The old church just across the road was forgotten and made into a school in 1715. Whilst being converted into a cottage in 1858, the discovery of two carved angels prompted the Revd Canon Jones to consult records in the Bodleian Library, Oxford, and confirm the re-discovery of the lost church of St Laurence.

The Walk

1. Go left from the railway station to take the Town Bridge across the River Avon. Bear left up Market Street. Turn left at the T-junction at its top and look for Conigre Hill on your right.

2. Go right up Conigre Hill. This lane becomes a footpath as it bears right and climbs to emerge on Winsley Road (the B3108) opposite Huntingdon Street. Go left along the pavement of Winsley Road. Turn left along Budbury Place, soon passing Budbury Circle on your right. Reach the top of forked steps overlooking the river and town. Fork right and keep right at a lower path junction. Look for steps descending on your left between houses. Take these to go down to a letterbox in the facing wall. Take the higher path on your right to visit St Mary's Chapel, Tory.

3. Retrace your steps to the letterbox and turn right down steps and along a path to a road (Newtown). Go left, then almost immediately down steps on the right to see the Ladywell. Turn left at the foot of these steps to pass the spring on your left and emerge from between houses on broad steps. Bear right down these, as signposted for the Saxon church. Reach St Laurence's Church on your left, passing Holy Trinity Church on your right. Cross a footbridge over the Avon.

4. Go right to pass the Riverside Inn on your left and take the path beside the river on your right past the swimming pool on your left. Follow the path under the railway bridge. Pass Barton Farm Tithe Barn on your left and take the path through the country park, near the river on your right. Go right around the Pump House for the Kennet and Avon Canal, then left along the path through meadows with the river on your right. Reach a weir. Go left up steps to the canal towpath and divert right to see the Avoncliff Aqueduct.

5. Retrace your steps to walk with the canal on your right back towards Bradford-on-Avon, passing the Tithe Barn on your left. Reach the Frome Road at the Canal Tavern.

6. Go left along the pavement of the Frome Road to return to the railway station, on your left.

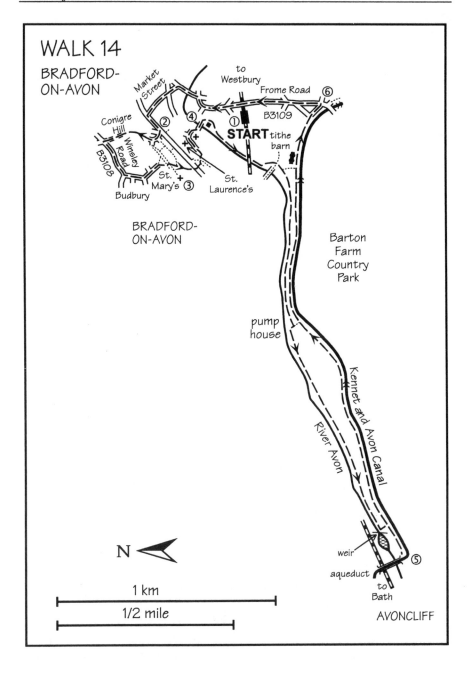

WALK 14
BRADFORD-
ON-AVON

Market Street

to Westbury

Frome Road ⑥

B3109

Conigre Hill

Winsley Road

B3108

② ④ ① **START** tithe barn

St. Mary's ③

St. Laurence's

Budbury

BRADFORD-
ON-AVON

Barton Farm Country Park

pump house

Kennet and Avon Canal

River Avon

N

1 km

1/2 mile

weir

aqueduct

⑤

to Bath

AVONCLIFF

15. DEVIZES

Route: Bishop's Cannings – Kennet and Avon Canal – Devizes

Distance: 4½ miles one way (linear walk with buses at each end). Easy.

Maps: OS Pathfinder 1185 Devizes and Marlborough, OS Landranger 173 Swindon and Devizes.

Start: Bus stop at the Crown Inn, Bishop's Cannings (SU037641).

Finish: Market Cross, Devizes (SUO04615).

Access: Buses run to Devizes from Salisbury (number 2), Chippenham (33), Swindon (49), Trowbridge (77) and Westbury (87). Telephone 0345 090899 for details. Bus number 49 serves Bishop's Cannings.

Ruth Pierce and the Moonrakers

Read the inscription on the market cross at the end of this walk in Devizes and be warned! It tells the story of Ruth Pierce, who agreed with three other women to buy a sack of wheat at the market on January 25th, 1753. They were each to contribute a fair share, but the money collected didn't add up to the required total. One of the other women accused Ruth Pierce of cheating. Ruth denied this and asked that God might strike her dead if she were lying. Repeating this wish, she fell down dead at the feet of a gathering crowd. The missing money was soon found clutched in her hand.

Those born in Wiltshire are known for being dim-witted rather than lying – 'Wiltshire born, Wiltshire bred, Wiltshire Folk are Thick in the Head'. It's not true, of course. They just like to give that impression. Never more so than when excise officers come searching for contraband. The famous story is of how excisemen caught smugglers in the act of reclaiming kegs of brandy from a pond in Bishop's Cannings. The men were skimming the surface of the water with their hay rakes when the officers asked them what they were doing. Quick as a flash, one replied that he was after 'thic gurt yaller cheese' (it was full moon). The officers saw the reflection of the moon in the water and concluded that the locals were poor, mad, 'moonrakers'. Moonrakers is now the proud name accepted by those born and bred in Wiltshire.

Wishing to find the actual pond where this legendary moonraking took place, I headed for Bishop's Cannings, where I met Laurence Wilshire. He claims to have the definitive story and gave me a copy of a report which he had deposited with Devizes Museum. The wise fools were his ancestors. The young Mr Wilshire heard the tale from his grandmother, a member of the Ruddle family. The Ruddles smuggled wool to Holland and returned with barrels of liquor in the 18th century. They were caught 'moonraking' at The Crammer, the large pond in Devizes, which was actually within the boundary of Bishop's Cannings parish in those days. Learn more about the Moonrakers at Devizes Museum (tel. 01380 727369).

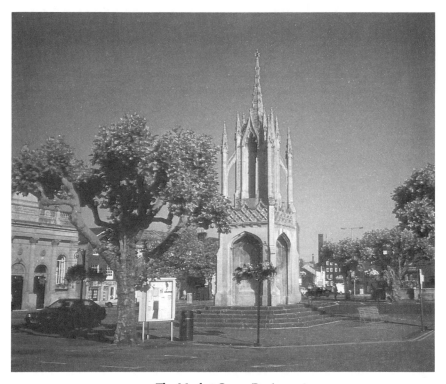

The Market Cross, Devizes

The Walk

1. With your back to the Crown Inn, Bishops Cannings, go right to St Mary's Church and turn right to take the path through the churchyard, passing the church on your left. Continue past thatched cottages in Church Walk. Turn right along a lane, as signposted for Horton.

2. When the lane ends, go ahead along a private concrete road which is a public path. Cross a swing-bridge over the Kennet and Avon Canal and turn right to walk along its towing path with the canal on your right. Pass under a road bridge at Horton, bridge 135, another road at Coate Bridge and bridge 137. Approach London Road Bridge at the outskirts of Devizes.

3. Fork left up a path to London Road and turn left along its pavement to pass St James's Church on your left. Continue to The Crammer (the Moonrakers' pond) on your left.

4. Go ahead up Sidmouth Street. Turn left along Sheep Street. Turn right up Morris Lane. Devizes Museum is across the road on your left. Continue by turning right along St John's Street to pass Castle Road, the Tourist Information Centre, then Castle Lane, on your left. The Market Cross is ahead on your right.

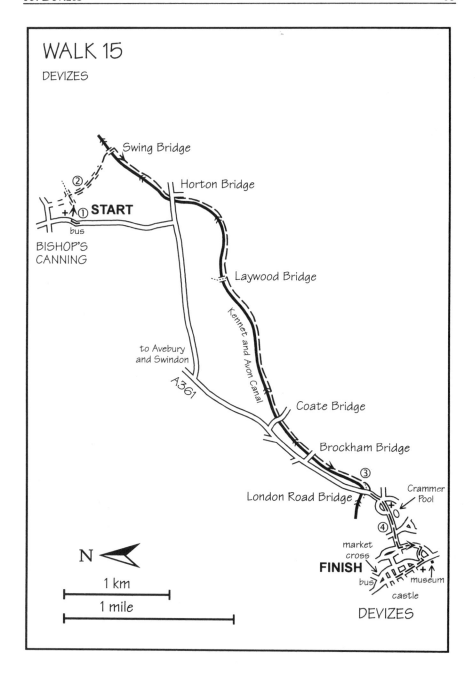

16. PEWSEY

Route: Pewsey — White Horse — Pewsey

Distance: 3½ miles. Strenuous.

Maps: OS Pathfinder 1185 Devizes and Marlborough and 1201 West Lavington, OS Landranger 173 Swindon and Devizes.

Start: The post office, Pewsey (SU164601).

Access: Buses to Pewsey include numbers 5 and 6 from Swindon and Salisbury. (Tel. 0345 090899 for details.) It is possible to arrive in Pewsey by train from London Paddington, Reading, Plymouth, Exeter and Westbury. (Tel. National Rail Enquiries 0345 484950.)

Pewsey White Horse

There is a record of a white horse here as long ago as 1785, so this may have been a traditional site for the emblem of the goddess Rhiannon. The current white horse was cut in 1937 by members of Pewsey Fire Brigade, under the direction of Mr George Marples, to celebrate the coronation of King George VI in 1937. Pewsey, like his birthplace at Wantage and his capital city of Winchester, can boast a statue of King Alfred the Great. He held land here, as well as fighting Guthrum's Danes not too far from here (see Walk 20, Kingston Deverill).

The Walk

1. With your back to the post office, go right and pass King Alfred's statue on your left. Go right, then left, along the pavement of the A345. Pass the church on your left, cross a bridge over the River Avon and leave the A345 by going straight ahead along Green Drove.

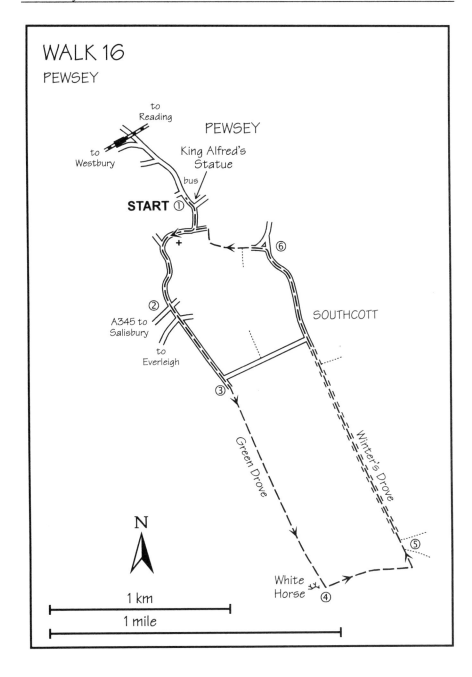

WALK 16
PEWSEY

to
Reading

PEWSEY

to
Westbury

King Alfred's
Statue

bus

START ①

+

⑥

②

A345 to
Salisbury

SOUTHCOTT

to
Everleigh

③

Green Drove

Winter's Drove

N

1 km

1 mile

White
Horse ④

⑤

2. Pass Everleigh Road on your right and Swan Meadow on your left.

3. When the road bends left, go straight ahead up a signposted bridleway towards Pewsey Hill. Cross a stile and climb the hillside to the white horse.

4. Climb to a stile above the white horse. Don't cross it! Go left to walk beside a fence on your right and with a view over the vale on your left. Cut across a coomb to rejoin the fence on your right and reach a stile in it. Bear left downhill to a stile in the bottom left corner.

5. Cross the stile and turn left along a grassy track (Winter's Drove), back to Pewsey. This becomes a firm track, joined by a track from your right. Go ahead along Southcott Road.

6. Fork left along Easterton Lane to pass the football ground on your right. Ignore a path on your left. Go right to walk upstream with the River Avon on your left. Turn left over a bridge and turn right along River Street to return to the start.

17. WESTBURY WHITE HORSE

Route: Westbury – Westbury White Horse – Westbury

Distance: 7 miles. Strenuous.

Maps: OS Pathfinder 1200 Westbury and Trowbridge, OS Landrangers 183 Yeovil and Frome and 184 Salisbury.

Start: Railway station, Westbury (ST862519).

Access: Trains run to Westbury from London, Bristol, Bath, Salisbury, Taunton and Weymouth. Buses include the X4 (Bath to Salisbury). (Tel. 0345 484950 for National Rail Enquiries, 0345 090899 for bus information.)

Westbury White Horse

The exposed, windswept chalk escarpment with its sweeping views to the north from Bratton Camp is just the spot for a white horse to be cut in the turf. The Westbury horse is above a side coomb facing Westbury in the west. There has probably been a figure of a horse here for thousands of years and it would be a representation of the goddess Rhiannon. The original horse is said to have been accompanied by a crescent moon, thus clinching the connection with the goddess. The spirit of fertility, of life itself, must flow strongly here, especially at dawn and dusk, at new and full moon, at the solstices and equinoxes and at Samhain, Imbolc, Beltane and Lughnasadh.

There is a Neolithic long barrow within Bratton Camp, perhaps indicating that this was a sacred site long before it became an Iron Age hill fort. Dowsing around the eye of the white horse, I found the most important ley or spirit path to run north-south, interestingly linking Cold Harbour at grid reference ST898587 (not far from Hag Hill) with a tumulus at grid reference ST898503 on Four Hundred Down, south of the White Horse, through whose eye this ley goes. This line extends southwards through tumuli on Battlesbury hill fort (ST898456) and on to the long barrow and tumuli at Bishop-strow (ST898444).

Alfred Watkins writes about the connection between Cold Harbour place names and leys in his seminal work *The Old Straight Track*. The 'Cold' element of the place name is from 'Coel', an omen. There is also a link with 'coal' and 'glow', and a presumption that beacons were lit at these places.

> *'Silver John is dead and gone*
> *And buried in Cole Harbour.'*

Clearly, the White Horse marks a potent, magical spot, recognised as sacred in the mists of prehistory. More mundane observers recall King Alfred gained a victory over the Danes at nearby Ethandun (now Edington) in 878. Perhaps this inspired a celebratory re-cutting which has lived long in local memory. An existing horse was remodelled by a Mr Gee in 1778, marking the ninth centenary of King Alfred's battle. A drawing of the original horse shows it facing the opposite direction to the present horse, and the crescent moon addition is at the end of a long, thin tail. Mr Gee's figure is unlike authentic ancient white horses (of Uffington, for example, visited in *Walks in Mysterious Oxfordshire*) in having the outline of a conventional horse-figure.

The Walk

1. Bear left along the station access road and pass a lake on your right. Go ahead under a railway bridge and along Station Road. Bear left at West End to reach the market square. Pass this on your right to continue along Alfred Street, which bears right to a crossroads. Go left along the pavement of the B3098 towards Bratton.

2. Fork left along a signposted bridleway. This provides views of the White Horse carved on a hillside on your right. Reach a road at a bend.

3. Turn right up the road, continue across the B3098 and climb with a signposted bridleway ahead. Walk with a hedge on your

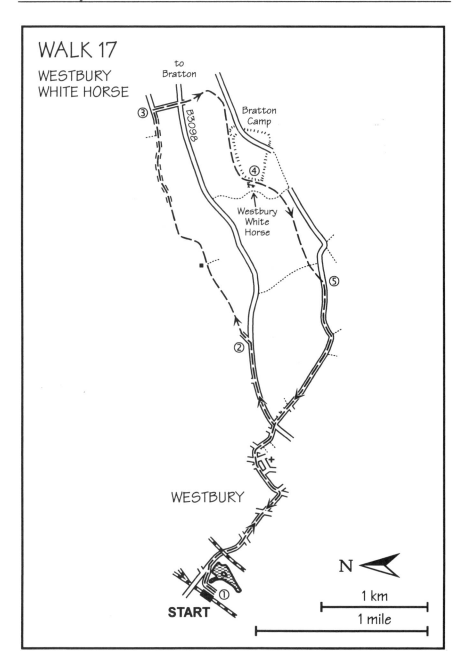

WALK 17
WESTBURY
WHITE HORSE

to
Bratton

③

B3098

Bratton
Camp

④

Westbury
White
Horse

⑤

②

WESTBURY

①
START

N

1 km
1 mile

left and bear right near the top to come to the earthworks of the hill fort known as Bratton Camp. Walk along its northern edge, overlooking the vale down on your right.

4. Continue from the top of the coomb above the White Horse to gain a view of the carved hill-figure by looking back from a toposcope at an altitude of 754 feet above sea level. Go ahead along the ridge, overlooking the cement works in the vale on your right. This path is waymarked with the dragon symbol of the Wessex Ridgeway. Continue over a stile and walk with a fence on your right. Go ahead over a second stile and eventually cross a third stile to gain access to a road.

Wembury White Horse

5. Go right down the road to return to Westbury and retrace your steps through the town to the railway station.

```
┌─────────────────────────────────────────────┐
│  ║                                         ║  │
│  ║            18. WARMINSTER              ║  │
│  ║                                         ║  │
└─────────────────────────────────────────────┘
```

Route: Warminster – Cradle Hill – Battlesbury hill fort – Warminster

Distance: 7½ miles. Strenuous.

Maps: OS Pathfinder 1220 Warminster, OS Landrangers 183 Yeovil and Frome and 184 Salisbury.

Start: Warminster railway station (ST877453).

Access: Trains run to Warminster from Bath, Westbury, Salisbury and further afield. (Tel. National Rail Enquiries 0345 484950.) Buses serving Warminster include the X4 (Bath to Salisbury), the number 53 (from Frome) and X77 (from Devizes). (Tel. 0345 090899 for details.)

The Warminster Triangle

The Iron Age hill fort at Battlesbury featured in the campaign between King Alfred the Great's Saxons and Guthrum's Danes in 878 (see Walk 20, Kingston Deverill). The second half of the 20th century has brought more intriguing scenes, of strange lights in the sky, UFOs (unidentified flying objects) or 'flying saucers'. Before dismissing such things, consult the record of them in The *Warminster Triangle* by Ken Rogers (with a foreword by the Marquess of Bath). It is hard not to conclude that there is something very mysterious about the Warminster area, or at least in its skies at night. Cradle Hill features greatly in the collection of reports, with references to it on 73 pages of Ken Rogers' book. There are 16 references to Battlesbury hill fort. Keep one eye on the sky whilst walking here!

The Walk

1. With your back to the railway station entrance, go right and right again under the railway bridge, then ahead along an enclosed path. Cross the road to take a path ahead up Cop Heap. At the foot of steps, fork left over a stile and climb before bearing left to a road. Go left along this for 50 metres.

Looking towards Scratchbury Hill Fort

2. Turn sharply right up the lane for the West Wilts Golf Club. Fork right, as signposted, to pass beside a garage and take a hedged path that bears left between the golf course on your left and Kidnapper's Hole on your right. Keep close to the fence on your right, eventually bearing right with the path. Pass a signposted bridleway going left. Take the signposted Imber Range Path ahead, keeping near the fence on your right, towards trees.

3. Turn right off the Imber Range Path along a signposted bridleway which is a metalled lane. Reach a lane junction on Cradle Hill and go right to pass Parsonage Farm on your left. Turn left with the signposted Imber Range Path, down a lane to Elm Hill.

4. Turn left along the pavement of a road, as signposted for the Imber Range Path. Pass the Army's School of Infantry on your left. Climb past Roberts of Kandahar Road on your left.

5. Turn right with the Imber Range Path and climb steps to a stile. Cross this to follow the waymarked Wessex Ridgeway, bearing

WALK 18
WARMINSTER

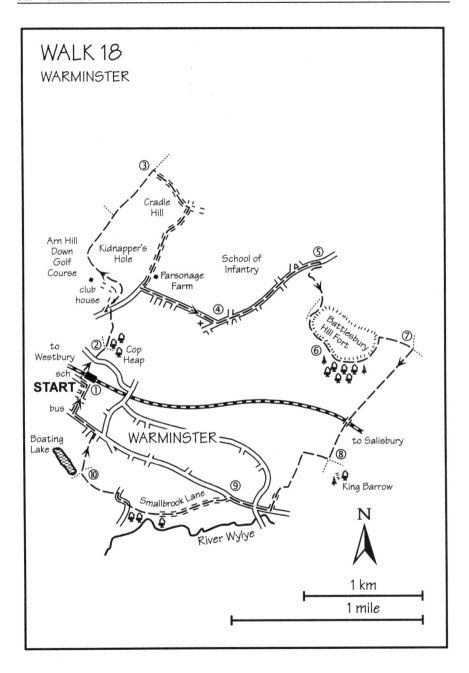

③

Cradle
Hill

Arn Hill
Down
Golf
Course

Kidnapper's
Hole

School of
Infantry

⑤

club
house

Parsonage
Farm

④

Battlesbury
Hill Fort

⑦

to
Westbury

②

Cop
Heap

⑥

sch

START ①

bus

to Salisbury

Boating
Lake

WARMINSTER

⑧

⑩

King Barrow

⑨

Smallbrook Lane

River Wylye

N

1 km

1 mile

right around the right-hand edge of a field. Cross a stile in the top right corner and bear right to pass the ramparts of Battlesbury hill fort on your left. Walk along the top of the outer rampart, ignoring a path descending on your right.

6. Take a stile into the woodland and emerge, still on top of the outer rampart. Bear left to meet a fence and descend to cross a stile waymarked as the Wessex Ridgeway. Turn right and descend over a stile beside a gate and a fence on your right.

7. Turn right off the Imber Range Path at a signposted crosspaths. Cross the railway by a bridge, reach a crosspaths and look for the tree-clad King Barrow in the field (with a gate) ahead on your left.

8. Turn right to follow a path which bends left to join a lane leading to a road. Go right along Boreham Road. Pass Bishopstrow Road on your left, then Woodcock Road on your right.

9. Bear left along Smallbrook Lane. Follow the path past woodland on your left. Go right at a road. When it bears right, take the hedged track ahead, passing Smallbrook Meadows on your left. Reach the gate for the boating lake, but don't take it!

10. Turn right up steps, then fork left along a narrow path to a road. Go left, then turn right along Station Road to return to the railway station.

```
┌─────────────────────────────────────────────────┐
│  ╔═════════════════════════════════════════════╗  │
│  ║                                             ║  │
│  ║            19. STONEHENGE                   ║  │
│  ║                                             ║  │
│  ╚═════════════════════════════════════════════╝  │
└─────────────────────────────────────────────────┘
```

Route: Stonehenge – New King Barrows – Old King Barrows – The Cursus – Stonehenge

Distance: 5 miles. Easy.

Maps: OS Pathfinder 1221 Shrewton, OS Landranger 184 Salisbury.

Start: Stonehenge (SU122423).

Access: Bus number 3 runs to Stonehenge from Salisbury, where it connects with trains at the railway station. Telephone 01722 336855 for more information about this service, or 0345 090899 for details of all buses and trains in Wiltshire.

The Temple of the Hyperboreans?

Written records didn't intrude into British history until the coming of the Romans. As a result, our ignorance of the past can easily be translated into a belief that the past was ignorant. Then we are confronted with Stonehenge. An example of conventional thought processes is that when the carving of a dagger showing remarkable similarity to daggers found in Mycenae was found on Stone 53, or when segmented faience beads were found in the barrows surrounding Stonehenge, as have been found at Mycenae, it may be presumed that there was a cultural flow from Greece, the centre of the classical world, to Britain, or Albion in those days. The suggestion that an island on the north-west fringe of Europe could have been of great importance in itself seems absurd. Yet there is evidence in the very writing of those classical Greeks that they were introduced to the worship of Apollo by the Hyperboreans who lived on an island which was, it seems, Britain.

Is Stonehenge the temple of Apollo? Diodorus, who wrote in the first century BC but referred to accounts that were ancient even in the days of Hecateus, around 500BC, wrote that 'the god visits the island every nineteen years, the period in which the re-turn of the stars to the same place in the heavens is accomplished, and for this reason the nineteen year period is called by Greeks the "year of Meton"'. Diodorus goes on to link this divine appearance 'from the vernal equinox until the rising of the Pleiades', which would make sense in 2000BC, when the Pleiades would have risen at the same time as the sun at the vernal equinox.

The 'year of Meton' (Meton was a Greek astronomer who discovered the Metonic cycle, whereby the full moon occurs on the same calendar date every nineteen years) may well have been discovered in Britain well over 1000 years before Meton. Nineteen years is also an approximation of 18.61, a figure which exercised Gerald Hawkins, author of *Stonehenge Decoded*, being the number of years in the cycle of regression of the lunar nodes. Three such cycles approximates to 56, which is the number of Aubrey Holes at Stonehenge, indicating that they could have been used to predict eclipses. Mathematicians, astronomers and engineers can have field days at Stonehenge, all testifying to the wonders and uniqueness of the site.

A replica of Stonehenge built elsewhere would not work. The importance of the place and its link with the Preselis, the hills in Pembrokeshire from which the bluestones were quarried, becomes apparent when reading the excellent book *A Key to Stonehenge* by Robin Heath. This author shows how Stonehenge was built to demonstrate harmony between patriarchal and matriarchal values. Its demise seems to have coincided with the rise of patriarchy, while today the monument is more like an internment camp than a sacred temple.

The first phase of Stonehenge was the construction of the henge, or outer ditch and bank, plus the circle of 56 Aubrey Holes within this, sometime around 2900BC. The second phase came in about 2100BC with the erection of bluestones at the centre of the henge, the addition of the Avenue and the significant placing of four Station Stones. The Station Stones formed a rectangle which can only be related to the solar and lunar alignments at this latitude (cf Hawkins' and Heath's books). The many barrows in the vicinity of Stonehenge, containing burials, also date from this time, which is interesting when the legend of the bluestones is considered.

The distinctive sarsen circle, with lintels accurately interlocked and jointed, forming a perfectly level circumference, date from Phase 3A, around 2000BC. Inside the sarsen circle was a sarsen horseshoe and the bluestones were re-erected in an oval within this by about 1550BC (Phase 3B). The bluestones were soon moved (Phase 3C) to form an oval between the sarsen horseshoe and circle, plus a second horseshoe within the larger one. Finally (Phase 4), the Avenue was extended sometime around 1100BC. Some say that the invading Romans deliberately damaged the temple because it was a source of power to their druidical opponents.

The connection between the Druids and Stonehenge is a controversial one, with critics stating that the site would have been a neglected ruin by the time that Druids were worshipping in oak groves (and not in stone temples), before the Romans added Britain to their empire in the first century AD. Modern Druids claim otherwise and demand their right to worship at Stonehenge when the sun rises at the summer solstice is on a par with Christmas in Salisbury Cathedral for Christians.

This matter of the antiquity of the druidical connection with Stonehenge may lead to a reappraisal of the Druids. One thing we do know about them is that they had phenomenal memories. They had

Druids celebrating the summer solstice at Stonehenge

no need for written records. When we gained what appears to be the convenience of writing, we lost the ability to remember to such a degree. Every gain brings its loss. It is perfectly possible for the memories of events to have been kept alive for thousands of years, and for Druids or their predecessors to have worshipped at Stonehenge.

When the legendary history of Stonehenge was first written down by Geoffrey of Monmouth in 1136, he had reason to link it with the Ambrosius Aurelianus who fought against the Saxons in the fifth century, as recorded by Gildas in the sixth century. This British ruler, whom Geoffrey named Aurelius Ambrosius, and whose name may have something to do with Amesbury, near Stonehenge and, even, the ancient name for Stonehenge, wanted to erect a monument to the 460 British nobles who had been treacherously slain at a feast by the Saxon allies of Vortigern. Stonehenge was to be that monument. So far, so bad, as Stonehenge was already ancient by the sixth century AD (when it would hardly have been 'safe' territory for the Saxons to massacre the British at a supposedly friendly feast – Hengest would have done better by inviting the British chieftains to Kent).

Geoffrey of Monmouth went on to record how Myrddin (better known to the English as Merlin) advised Ambrosius to bring the 'Giants' Dance' from Killaraus, a mountain in Ireland. As recently as 1923 it was discovered that the bluestones must have come from Carn Menyn, in the Preselis. These Pembrokeshire hills were considered Irish territory in the fifth century. Did Geoffrey know something?

As Robin Heath writes, 'it cannot have been much fun to have dragged and floated .. megaliths from West Wales to Salisbury Plain', and his book *A Key to Stonehenge* does give compelling reasons for the project. Your author, too, can contribute a dream he recorded on Carn Ingli, Pembrokeshire, which seemed to be of a circle of bluestones standing on the plateau below Foel Drygarn in the Preselis. Giants have also featured in the Carn Ingli dreams (and can be discerned in the landscape still), so was this the 'Giants' Dance'?

Myrddin, like Arthur, is an archetypal figure who recurs throughout history. So there may well have been a Myrddin (and an Aurelius Ambrosius) in the Bronze Age, as W.A. Cummins postulates in his book *King Arthur's Place in Prehistory – The Great Age of Stonehenge*. Ancient Albion's King Arthur may have gripped the imagination so that his fame spread all over Europe, rather than being confined to a sixth-century Briton's struggles against the Saxons. Are we back with the Hyperboreans?

Leys, or spirit paths, radiate from, or converge on, Stonehenge. One very important ley runs virtually south through Old Sarum and Salisbury Cathedral to Clearbury. Sir Norman Lockyer noted this alignment before Alfred Watkins wrote his seminal book The *Old Straight Track*. Paul Devereux and Ian Thomson detail it in their book *The Ley Hunter's Companion*, while this ley's extension to Frankenbury Camp features in my *Walks in Mysterious Hampshire*. This ley is met again in Walk 22 (Salisbury Cathedral) of this book. Paul Devereux has written much about the Stonehenge Cursus, including identifying a ley running along it, through Woodhenge and, perhaps, eastwards to Beacon Hill.

The Walk

1. After visiting Stonehenge, go to the far end of its car park and go left along a track to the A344. Cross this road and continue with the track ahead (Druids' Lodge Track). Cross the A303 and go ahead along the signposted track.

2. Turn left over a stile beside a gate to take a signposted path which follows the right-hand edge of a field with a line of barrows on your right. Continue over a stile, across Wilsford Track and another stile. Walk along a National Trust path with a fence running along your right. Continue by crossing a stile ahead.

3. Turn left, as waymarked in the corner of the field. Follow a fence on your right, go ahead over a stile in the corner and turn left to walk with a fence on your left. Take a waymarked gap in the corner and pass trees on your right. When level with the end of this woodland, bear left downhill.

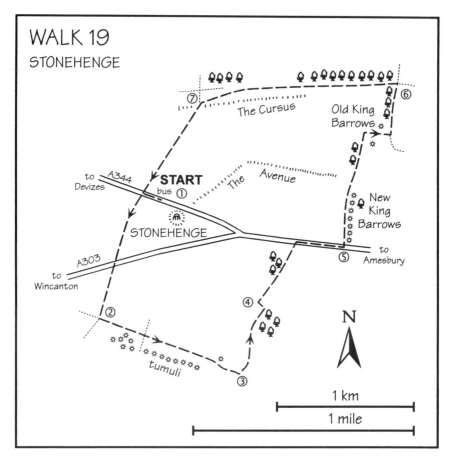

WALK 19

STONEHENGE

4. Turn right when four fields meet and walk up a track to pass more trees on your left. **(There is a tumulus under these trees.)** Reach the A303, go right and follow the cycle track until reaching trees across the road on your left.

5. Turn left across the road and go ahead through a waymarked gate to walk along a grass track past the New King Barrows, under the trees on your right. Pass a stile on your left at the Avenue. Continue past trees on your left. Follow a broad, fenced track as it bends right and pass the Old King Barrows. Turn left at a track junction and pass more trees on your left.

6. Turn left along the track to the Cursus. Cross a stile to walk along the edge of the Cursus, with a line of trees on your right. Continue over a stile to the right of a gate in a fence ahead. Go ahead beside a fence on your right and cross another stile beside a gate. Reach more trees on your right. Bear left to a stile in the fence ahead and cross it.

7. Turn left along a track to leave the Cursus and return to the car park and bus terminus at Stonehenge.

20. KINGSTON DEVERILL

Route: Kingston Deverill – Egbert's Stone – Court Hill – White Sheet Hill – Kingston Deverill

Distance: 8½ miles. Strenuous.

Maps: OS Pathfinder 1240 Mere, OS Landranger 183 Yeovil and Frome.

Start: St Mary's Church, Kingston Deverill (ST846371).

Access: I came here by Wessex Taxis from Warminster (tel. 01985 218988/212435 or freephone 0800 801245). Trains and buses run to Warminster. (Tel. 0345 090899 for details.)

England's Stone of Destiny

Not so long ago our ancestors recognised that certain stones in special places (or, clearly, brought from some distance to a particular spot, suggesting that both stone and place have value) could impart some magic. When King Alfred the Great was in desperate straits, with Wessex invaded by Guthrum's Danes in 878, this descendant of Cerdic (and, therefore, of the ancient British rulers of this land whose name is derived from the Gewissei tribe and not, as supposed, from any West Saxons) moved out of his winter refuge at Athelney in Somerset, he followed the firm track of Harrow Way eastwards through the formidable barrier of Selwood Forest to *Ecghryhsstan*, or Egbert's Stone. Alfred was the grandson of King Egbert.

This fabled stone is where Alfred came for inspiration before he gained what has been described as the most important victory ever won on English soil. Egbert's Stone is where Alfred assembled his army, with men coming from Somerset, Wiltshire and the western half of Hampshire (but not from Dorset, where they were presumably needed to guard the coastline). Alfred needed a sheltered, well-drained area for his men to camp at while the Saxon army assembled with the security of concealment. Kingston Deverill is such a location, while strong local oral tradition states that Alfred came here before his victory over the Danes. This route starts out along an ancient path (with eight tumuli near it) which linked Kingston Deverill with the Harrow Way or Hard Way at White Sheet Hill. The Roman road from Poole to Bath and the old Roman 'Lead' road also converge here, making it the ideal site for Alfred to rally his troops. With Guthrum concentrating his army in a defensive position astride the route to Chippenham, selecting the high ground around Bratton Castle (Walk 17), Alfred continued to Iley Oak (Robin Hood's Bower, ST877423) and the next day to Edington.

Rather than a single stone, there were three stones, two leaning against each other with the third serving as a capstone. They stood near the first tumulus passed on this walk on Court Hill (like King's Hill, to the south of the village, an interesting name). They were brought down by the farmer with a view to breaking them up to use as road-stone. Proving to be too hard, they ended up in the field to the west of the church, where the two leaning uprights can still be seen. The capstone was used by men of the USAF to cover a dump of ammunition which is buried nearby (and is live, so tread carefully!).

Egbert's Stone?

What symbolism at the end of the Second World War! Urgent priority should now be given to recovering the capstone and re-erecting these stones on Court Hill.

The Walk

1. With your back to St Mary's Church, go left and soon turn left, as signposted for Maiden Bradley. Notice Egbert's Stone in the field on your left. Return to the church and continue past it on your right, taking a lane away from the main road. Go ahead along a no through road.

2. Turn left along a concrete track and immediately turn right through a gate to take the bridleway signposted for White Sheet Hill. Go straight ahead to take a waymarked gate and then another. Walk beside a fence on your left. When this fence bears left, go ahead to pass below a tumulus on your left. Pass the end of a belt of woodland on your left and take a gate in a fence ahead. Pass the trees of Peter's Penning on your left.

3. Turn left through a gate waymarked with a blue arrow. Walk with a fence on your right for 250 metres, then turn right through a waymarked gate. Bear slightly left through a field to take another waymarked gate and continue along a grass track between fields.

4. Go ahead across a track, through a gate and beside a fence on your right. Continue with a fence on your left in the next field. Reach a fenced track (the Harrow Way) and turn right along it. Divert left through a gate giving access to White Sheet Castle. Go ahead to a gate to the left of water reservoirs and a radio mast. A second gate gives admission to the earthworks of this hill fort.

5. Retrace your steps to the Harrow Way, cross it and take the gate opposite. Bear left, as waymarked, to follow a bridleway to White Sheet Down. Ignore a stile in the fence on your right. As the fence bears right, go ahead through the plateau and take a path on the

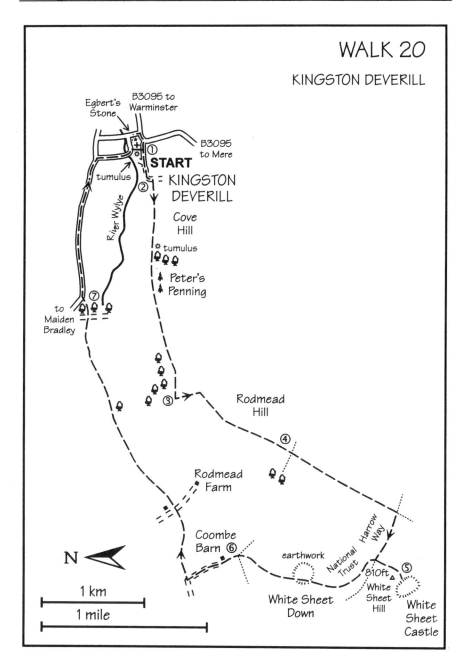

WALK 20

KINGSTON DEVERILL

Egbert's Stone

B3095 to Warminster

B3095 to Mere

① START

= KINGSTON DEVERILL

②

tumulus

River Wylye

Cove Hill

☀ tumulus

Peter's Penning

to Maiden Bradley

⑦

③

Rodmead Hill

④

Rodmead Farm

Coombe Barn ⑥

earthwork

National Trust

Harrow Way

810ft

⑤

White Sheet Hill

White Sheet Down

White Sheet Castle

N

1 km

1 mile

right-hand side of a final spur to descend and take a gate in the left-hand corner giving access to a track.

6. Turn left along the fenced track, soon passing farm buildings on your right. Continue along a hedged lane until this bends left. Turn right through a gate to walk with a hedge on your left through two fields. Cross a lane and continue along the left-hand edges of four more fields. Pass a small triangle of woodland on your right. Emerge along the right-hand edge of a field, then along the left-hand edge of the next field. Cross a track and go ahead through two gates.

7. Pass a tumulus on your left as you enter a field. Go straight ahead to a stile beside a gate and a signpost to reach a road. Go right along this and turn right after about one mile. Cross a bridge over the River Wylye at Kingston Deverill. Go left and almost immediately turn right through the gate of number 36. Pass this cottage and its garden on your right. Continue through a gate to pass a field with a tumulus on your right. Follow the path through the churchyard to return to the start.

21. GROVELY WOOD

Route: Stoford Bridge—Great Wishford—Roman road—Grovely Wood—Great Wishford—Stoford Bridge

Distance: 5½ miles. Moderate.

Maps: OS Pathfinder 1241 Salisbury (North), OS Landranger 184 Salisbury.

Start: Stoford Bridge (SU083355).

Access: Buses numbers 2 (Salisbury to Shrewton and Devizes) and X4 (Salisbury to Bath) stop at Stoford Bridge. (Tel. 0345 090899 for details.)

May Queens

Go to Salisbury Cathedral on May 29th to see the annual dance celebrating the freedom of local people to collect dead wood from Grovely Wood. To cries of 'Grovely, Grovely, Grovely, all Grovely', four ladies, representing four women who defied the Earl of Pembrokeshire in the 19th century when he tried to stop them gathering sticks so that his pheasants wouldn't be disturbed, carry 'nitches' (bundles of dry sticks) into the Cathedral. A charter dating from 1603 is read from the high altar. The four women who defied their lord of the manor suffered a day in prison before the authorities were forced to recognise that they were enjoying an ancient privilege and released them. Grace Reed, Fanny Pomeroy, Ann Hibberd and Sarah Abraham were the four heroines. The local men had been too afraid to disobey the Earl of Pembroke. May 29th was King Charles II's birthday, the day when he rode through London to mark the restoration of the monarchy in 1660, and Oak Apple Day, when celebrations are led by the May Queen. Great Wishford church was where the baptisms took place of seven children delivered at one birth in the 15th century to Lady Edith Bonham, wife of Sir Thomas Bonham.

The Walk

1. From the bus stop on the main road, cross Stoford Bridge over the River Wylye to follow the road to Great Wishford. Reach the church and go left along South Street. Continue past Grovely Cottages, numbers 22 to 27 (the first turning on your left).

2. Turn right to take the track under the railway bridge and uphill. Continue through woodland. Go ahead at a first crosstracks for 200 metres to reach a waymarked second crosstracks.

3. Turn right along a firm track (the Roman road which linked Bath with Old Sarum), now known as First Broad Drive. When this tree-lined avenue bends right, take the path straight ahead to Grovely Wood.

4. Turn right along a firm lane signposted as a bridleway (this is Grovely Road). Descend with it to Great Wishford. Continue along West Street, passing the church on your right. Retrace your steps to the bus stops.

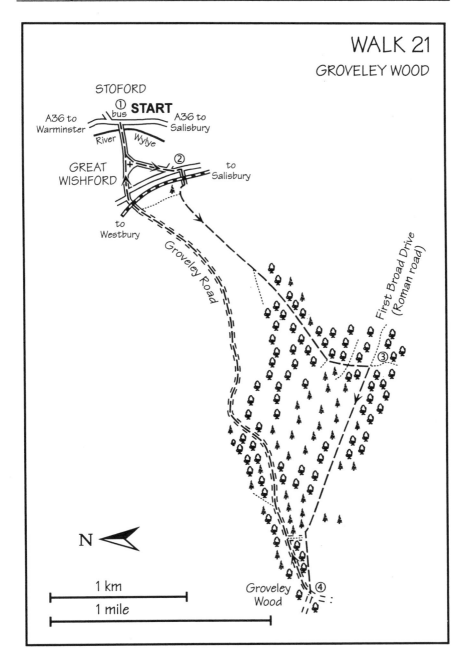

WALK 21
GROVELEY WOOD

STOFORD
① START
bus

A36 to
Warminster
A36 to
Salisbury

River Wylye

GREAT
WISHFORD
②
to
Salisbury

to
Westbury

Groveley Road

First Broad Drive
(Roman road)

③

N

1 km
1 mile

Groveley
Wood
④

22. WINTERSLOW

Route: Middle Winterslow — Roman road — The Pheasant Hotel — East Winterslow — Middle Winterslow

Distance: 5 miles. Moderate.

Maps: OS Pathfinder 1242 The Wallops, OS Landranger 184 Salisbury.

Start: Lion's Head pub, The Common, Middle Winterslow (SU245326).

Access: Bus number 68 (Salisbury to Winchester) stops near the Lion's Head pub in Middle Winterslow. There is a request stop for bus number 76 (Salisbury to Basingstoke) at the Pheasant Hotel (direction point 5). Telephone 0345 090899 for bus times.

An Attack by a Lioness and much more

The Pheasant Hotel used to be called The Hut and was a favourite resort of the essayist William Hazlitt. It was what happened on the evening of Sunday, 20 October, 1816, that is most recalled in these parts, however. A contemporary picture of the event hangs near the bar of the hotel. It shows a lioness attacking the offside leading horse of the Exeter to London mail coach. The guard was about to aim his blunderbuss at her when a menagerie owner shouted to stop him and managed to retrieve the lioness with the aid of his dog. The passengers took shelter in the inn until the beast was securely loaded in its caravan and taken to Salisbury Fair. The wounded horse, Pomegranate, had to be replaced, with his owner receiving compensation and the magistrates ordering the menagerie owner to secure his dangerous creatures safely.

There is a spirit to the Winterslow area that makes it an appropriate venue for the lioness's bid for freedom. Thomas Boulter, the highwayman, held up the Exeter mail coach at The Hut in the 1770s, making the passengers hand over all their money. He was finally captured and sentenced to death in 1778.

Winterslow was also famous for a witch. She used to turn herself into a hare and confound the hounds by leading them astray. A farmer shot the hare with a silver bullet, as advised by the Rector of Tytherley. The wounded hare managed to reach the witch's cottage before expiring. Lyddie Shears was the unfortunate woman's name, and she had been known to assist poachers by mesmerising the hares. Perhaps it is her ghost which explains the headless woman seen on the Roman road near Middle Winterslow.

The Collins family from Winterslow were expert truffle hunters. Their dogs were descended from Spanish poodles. A truffle was once presented to Queen Victoria, who sent a photograph and a golden sovereign in payment. The old custom of mumming plays lived on until relatively recently in Winterslow. The mummers acted out the story of St George, involving a Turkish Knight and a Doctor.

The Walk

1. Face the Lion's Head pub and take the signposted byway on your left, which takes you past the pub on your right. Reach a children's playground.

2. Bear left with the old Roman road. Pass the access lane to Cooper's Farm on your right. Continue along the metalled Roman road to join the main road through the village.

3. As you approach a small junction, turn sharply right along a narrow, hedged path. Emerge over a stile and continue along the right-hand edge of a field. Pass a stile in the fence on your right. Go ahead over a stile in the corner and continue with a fence on your right. Cross a stile in the next corner and turn left along an old green lane.

4. Go ahead across a road. Descend with the old green lane to another road and bear right along it.

5. Turn right along the verge of the A30, passing the Pheasant Hotel on your left. Turn right over a stile to follow the signposted path along the left-hand edge of a field.

6. Pass Gutteridge Farm on your right and continue along the left-hand edge of the next field. Cross a stile to keep climbing along the left-hand edge of the following field. The right of way continues over a stile and past a patch of woodland on your right to reach a road. This path was made most unpleasant by tall nettles in July 1997 so I made an unofficial diversion, bearing right to a gate and going left along a road to reach the far end of the 'nettle' path at a road junction. Take the road signposted for Winterslow for 50 metres.

7. Turn right over a stile beside a gate and follow the signposted footpath through fields to rejoin the outward route at the old green lane. This time turn left, downhill. Go ahead at the first track junction.

8. Turn right at the next junction, where you can see a telephone box down the lane ahead. Descend to where the children's playground is on your right and turn left to retrace your steps to the Lion's Head pub.

WALK 22
WINTERSLOW

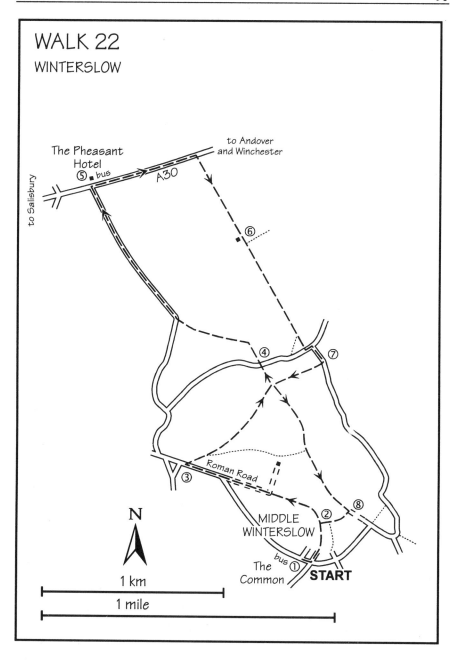

The Pheasant Hotel
⑤ bus
A30
to Salisbury
to Andover and Winchester
⑥
④
⑦
Roman Road
③
N
1 km
1 mile
MIDDLE WINTERSLOW
② ⑧
The Common
bus ①
START

23. SALISBURY CATHEDRAL

Route: Old Sarum – Salisbury Cathedral

Distance: 5 miles one way (linear route with bus stops at each end). Easy.

Maps: OS Pathfinders 1241 Salisbury (North) and 1262 Salisbury (South), OS Landranger 184 Salisbury.

Start: Old Sarum bus stop (SU141325).

Finish: Salisbury Cathedral (SU143296).

Access: Trains and buses come to Salisbury from all directions. Buses numbers 3, 5, 6, 7, 8 and 9 stop at Old Sarum. Telephone 0345 090899 for information about buses and trains in Wiltshire.

A Divine Bow Shot

Old Sarum and Salisbury Cathedral are both on a ley or spirit path running south from Stonehenge (Walk 19) to Clearbury Ring (see Walk 26 Odstock). This is a well-documented alignment, featuring in *The Ley Hunter's Companion* by Paul Devereux and Ian Thomson. Stand on the southern rim of Old Sarum to see the line of this ley pass the eastern side of the cathedral spire and clip the western edge of Clearbury's wooded hill fort.

Old Sarum was continuously inhabited from at least the Iron Age to the Middle Ages, with a cathedral started by Bishop Herman in 1078 and the final version (the first being all but destroyed in a storm just five days after its consecration in 1092) completed by Bishop Roger in 1139. It didn't last long, ostensibly because of friction between the governors of the garrison (who held the keys of the city and once locked the dean and his clergy out one night) and the bishops. Bishop Poore petitioned Pope Honorius III for permission to erect a new cathedral in meadow land to the south so that the clergy could exercise their independence. The shortage of water, the windy nature of the hill fort and the glaring whiteness of its cliffs were also cited. More telling are the legends. One states that an archer drew his bow and fired an arrow which landed two miles due south, in a water-meadow visited at intervals by floods. A second legend is of the bishop obeying instructions received in a vision of the Virgin Mary. Ludicrous as it seemed, Bishop Poore proceeded to build the new cathedral on such an unlikely spot. Perhaps he knew of the ley and felt the urge to move the sacred site further down its line from Stonehenge. The legend of the bow shot is a classic case of location by divination. Salisbury Cathedral was consecrated in 1264, while its famous spire was added in the 14th century.

Guy Underwood, the dowser who wrote *The Pattern of the Past*,

Salisbury Cathedral

identified an exceptionally powerful blind spring in the centre line of the nave under the cathedral spire. The cathedral site had long been a junction of three hundreds, so was most probably marked in some way. The city of New Sarum (Salisbury)'s street patterns also relate to the line of the Stonehenge to Clearbury ley. Even the distances involved are curiously exact – from Stonehenge to Old Sarum being six miles, from Old Sarum to Salisbury Cathedral is two miles, while

Clearbury Ring is exactly three miles from Salisbury Cathedral. The cathedral spire is also visited by mysterious swarms of flying ants at times, and a white bird appears there whenever a Bishop of Salisbury is about to die.

Until 1832 elections for the 'Rotten Borough' of Old Sarum were held under a tree marked by the Parliament Stone, passed on this walk and sited on the ley. The Cathedral Close is home to the Salisbury Museum (tel. 01722 332151), the Royal Gloucestershire, Berkshire and Wiltshire Regiment Museum (tel. 01722 414556), Mompesson House (tel. 01722 335659), Malmesbury House (tel. 01722 327027) and the Medieval Hall (tel. 01722 412472), so allow plenty of time at the end of this walk to visit the cathedral and these nearby attractions.

The Walk

1. With your back to the bus stop (having taken the bus from Salisbury to Old Sarum), go left and turn left. Fork right to reach Old Sarum.

2. Retrace your steps to the fork and turn right (as if you had forked left when first here), as signposted for Stratford Sub-Castle. Walk beside a hedge on your right. Converge with a hedged path coming from your left and turn right down it. Pass the Parliament Stone on your right.

3. Go right at a road and when this bends right, turn left with an enclosed footpath. Continue past a school on your left and along Hulse Road. Turn right at Ashley Road to cross a bridge.

4. Turn left along the riverside walk, going downstream with the Avon on your left. Continue to Bishop's Mill.

5. Cross Fisherton Street to put the river on your right. Turn right over Crane Bridge, as signposted for the Riverside Walk. Turn left over a zebra crossing to continue with the river on your left again. Bear right with the path at a confluence and take a foot-

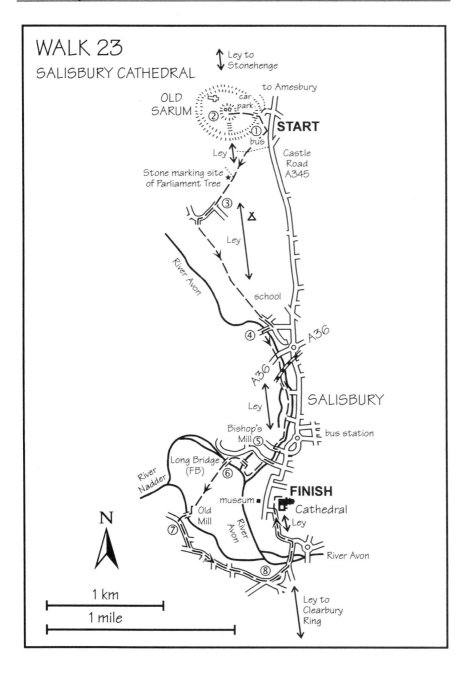

WALK 23
SALISBURY CATHEDRAL

Ley to Stonehenge

to Amesbury

OLD SARUM

car park

START

② ∞ bus

①

Castle Road A345

Ley

Stone marking site of Parliament Tree

③

Δ

Ley

River Avon

school

④

A36

A36

SALISBURY

Ley

Bishop's Mill ⑤

bus station

Long Bridge (FB) ⑥

River Nadder

museum ■

FINISH
Cathedral
Ley

Old Mill

⑦

River Avon

River Avon

⑧

Ley to Clearbury Ring

N

1 km

1 mile

bridge on your left. Bear left and turn left across another foot-bridge.

6. Follow the Town Path to reach Old Mill.

7. Bear left up Lower Street. Go left along Harnham Road.

8. Fork left, signposted for Harnham Road numbers 2-56 and 1-61. Cross the bridge over the river with St Nicholas Road and turn left along De Vaux Place, bending right at Broad Walk to reach Salisbury Cathedral.

24. ANSTY

Route: Tisbury – Ansty – Tisbury

Distance: 6 miles. Moderate.

Maps: OS Pathfinder 1261 Shaftesbury, OS Landranger 184 Salisbury.

Start: Tisbury railway station (ST945291).

Access: Tisbury is served by trains from Salisbury, London Waterloo, Yeovil and Exeter. Bus number 26 runs from Salisbury and Shaftesbury. Telephone 0345 090899 for details of trains and buses in Wiltshire or 0345 484950 for National Rail Enquiries.

Ansty Maypole

Maypoles used to be a familiar sight on village greens, remaining in place until signs of age demanded a replacement. Puritans disliked them and the merriment they occasioned so an Act of Parliament ordered their removal in 1644. This law was repealed after Charles II was restored to the throne, but the damage had been done. Ansty's maypole is a rare surviving example, especially in a road. The tall larch pole is garlanded with wildflowers collected from local woodland, ribbons are fastened to the pole and stallholders display their wares around it. A chair is set up for the May Queen to occupy. The floral crown is placed on her head by the retiring queen, while traditional tunes are played for dancers. The maypole is now renewed every 25 years for safety's sake. The road is closed to all traffic from midnight to noon when this happens.

The Walk

1. Bear right from the railway station and turn sharply right with a waymarked footpath. Fork right and cross the railway carefully.

Bear left to emerge over a stile in the bottom corner of a field. Bear left uphill, cross a stile and go left beside a fence on your left.

2. Go ahead over a stile in the corner and bear right through fields, crossing three stiles, to reach a road. Go right.

3. Turn left along a signposted bridleway, soon bearing left at a fork. Leave a private road at a gate by forking right with the way-marked bridleway (blue arrow). Follow the old holloway into woodland. Bear right to pass a cleared area on your left, and enter more woodland on the slopes of Castle Ditch hill fort.

4. Turn right at a woodland path junction and take a gate to bear left downhill. Walk with a fence on your left to reach a track. Go left and fork left to keep with the higher track, then bear right to descend through a gate.

5. Turn left through a gate to take a path into woodland. Don't take the first gate ahead out of this wood! Go right, inside the wood, to emerge in the corner of a field. Keep above a wooded slope on your right.

6. Bear right through a waymarked gate to descend to a lane. Bear left down this to a road at Swallowcliffe. Go right to pass the Royal Oak pub and the road for Salisbury on your left. Come to St Peter's Church on your right (visit it to see a rare grave slab of an abbess on the porch floor).

7. Turn left with a signposted footpath. Climb and turn left with an enclosed path. Go ahead over a stile beside a gate, through a field and across a stile in the middle of its fence. Bear right up to a stile giving access to a woodland path, which you take. Emerge over a stile and go ahead up a field. Cross a stile, go through a second field and over a stile beside a gate. Continue beside a hedge on your right, then go ahead with a hedged path. Turn left for 10 metres.

WALK 24

ANSTY

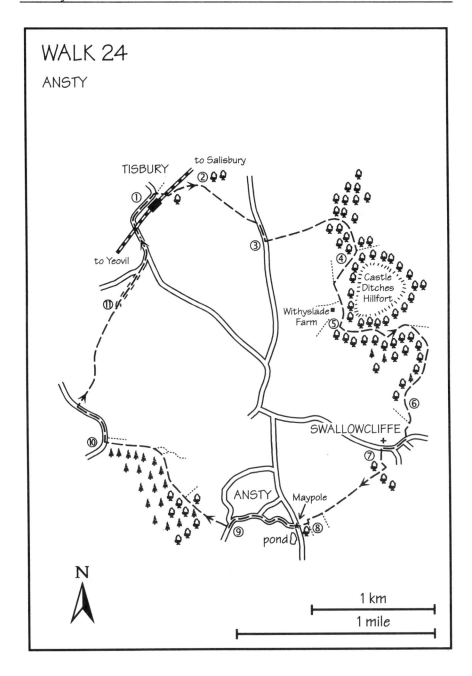

TISBURY

to Salisbury

to Yeovil

Castle
Ditches
Hillfort

Withyslade
Farm

SWALLOWCLIFFE

ANSTY

Maypole

pond

N

1 km

1 mile

8. Turn right down a steep, narrow path into Ansty. Go right for 10 metres to the maypole at a road junction. Turn left along the road signposted for Ansty Coombe. Pass two roads on your right and proceed for a further 40 metres.

9. Bear right through a gate and up a field to a stile in its top right corner. Cross the stile into woodland and bear right. Go ahead at a path junction to walk just inside the wood. Ignore a path on your right. Emerge on a road.

10. Go right down the road and soon pass a signposted footpath on your right. Reach the end of the second field on your right and turn right through a gate (the signpost is on the other side of the road). Walk along the left-hand edges of two fields, ahead through a third and reach a gate giving access to a track.

11. Take the track down to a road, where you go right and bear left at a junction to return to Tusbury.

25. FOVANT BADGES

Route: Broad Chalke – Fovant Down – Fovant – Chiselbury hill fort – Compton Down – Broad Chalke

Distance: 7 miles. Strenuous.

Maps: OS Pathfinder 1262 Salisbury (South), OS Landranger 184 Salisbury.

Start: Queen's Head pub, Broad Chalke (SU039256).

Access: Bus number 29 (Salisbury to Shaftesbury) stops near the Queen's Head pub in Broad Chalke. Buses numbers 26 and 27 (Salisbury to Shaftesbury or Hindon) stop in Fovant (direction point 6). Telephone 0345 090899 for details.

Chalk Insignia

The cluster of regimental badges on Fovant Down is said to be the largest group of hill carvings in Europe. Wiltshire's Nadder Valley became a huge army camp during the First World War, complete with rifle ranges, hospitals and a cinema. A railway was built to bring men in for training (some came from as far afield as Australia) and to take them off to the Western Front. German prisoners of war were held here too. The first regimental cap badge was cut by men of the 5th Battalion, London Rifle Brigade, early in 1916. By 1919 there were 20 badges spaced out along the downs between Sutton Mandeville and Compton Chamberlayne. These were cut very early in the mornings, before 0700 hours, so each badge represents months of effort, digging accurate trenches and filling them with chalk (the ones that were outlined by bricks were the badges that didn't survive). Some regiments paid local people to care for their badges after the war. Ironically, the Second World War almost saw their demise when the badges were grassed over to avoid becoming navigational aids to the Luftwaffe. They were spruced up after 1945 by Fovant Home Guard Old Comrades Association. Now the Fovant Badges Society looks after them, while there is a museum in the Pembroke Arms, Fovant. Twelve badges remain, allowing for three post-World War II additions.

The Walk

1. Face the Queen's Head and go left, then turn right with the village street. Pass no through roads on your left and right. When the street bends left, take a no through road ahead (signposted for Chalk Pit Farm).

2. Go through the farmyard and turn left along a signposted bridleway, soon bearing right along a hedged, grassy track.

3. Join a grassy track coming from your left and continue with a fence on your right along the grassy track between Gurston Down on your left and Knapp Down on your right. Take a gate to emerge on a ridgeway track. Cross this and a stile to follow a waymarked path down through scrubby woodland on the slope of Fovant Down.

4. Bear right when the path forks. Descend to a stile in the bottom fence, cross it and take the left-hand edge of the field down towards Fovant. Cross a stile in the bottom corner and go ahead to another stile giving access to lanes.

5. Go left into the village of Fovant. Pass the Cross Keys pub on your right and the Pembroke Arms, with its First World War Museum, on your left.

6. Walk along the pavement/cycle track of the A30 and pass a signposted footpath on your left. See the badges on your right. Turn right along a lane to East Farm (signposted as a public bridleway).

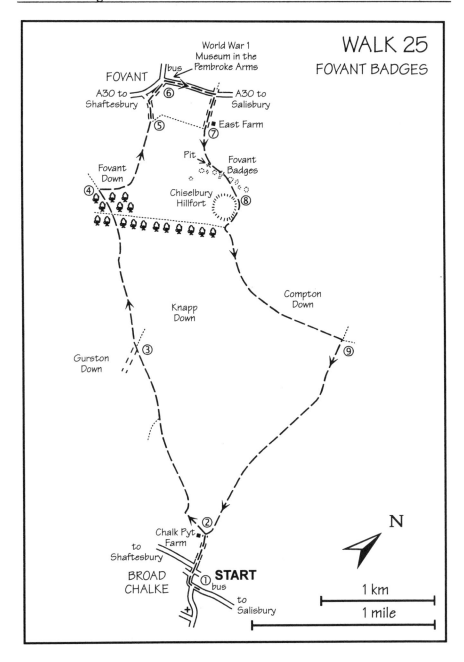

WALK 25
FOVANT BADGES

World War 1
Museum in the
Pembroke Arms

FOVANT

bus

A30 to
Shaftesbury

⑥

A30 to
Salisbury

⑤

East Farm

⑦

Pit

Fovant
Badges

Fovant
Down

④

Chiselbury
Hillfort

⑧

Compton
Down

Knapp
Down

Gurston
Down

③

⑨

②

Chalk Pyt
Farm

to
Shaftesbury

BROAD
CHALKE

① START
bus

to
Salisbury

N

1 km

1 mile

7. Take a waymarked gate ahead towards the badges. Cross a stile and bear left beside a chalk pit, soon climbing the slope to the badges. Pass a 'crown' top half of a badge on your right and climb to a stile in the top fence.

8. Go ahead to pass the ramparts of Chiselbury hill fort on your right. Continue over a stile to the left of a gate at the back of the hill fort and turn left along the ridgeway track.

9. Turn right at a junction with a bridleway to Chalk Pyt Farm. Retrace your steps into Broad Chalke.

```
┌─────────────────────────────────────────────────┐
│                                                   │
│                26. ODSTOCK                        │
│                                                   │
└─────────────────────────────────────────────────┘
```

Route: Odstock – Clearbury Ring – Odstock

Distance: 5½ miles. Moderate.

Maps: OS Pathfinder 1262 Salisbury (South), OS Landranger 184 Salisbury.

Start: Odstock crossroads (SU146261).

Access: Buses to Odstock include the X3 (Salisbury to Bournemouth) and number 29 (Salisbury to Shaftesbury). Telephone 0345 090899 for details.

Joshua Scamp's Grave

Buried in the churchyard of St Mary's, Odstock, are the remains of an old gypsy called Joshua Scamp. He was hanged in Salisbury on 1 April, 1801, after being found guilty of stealing a horse. In actual fact it was his son-in-law who had committed the capital offence. Joshua preferred to pay the ultimate penalty of being a devoted father, rather than see his daughter widowed. Felons were not usually allowed a churchyard burial, but the vicar was persuaded to allow Joshua to rest here and his tombstone is accompanied by a rambler rose.

Gypsies made an annual pilgrimage to Joshua's grave on the anniversary of his death. Unfortunately, this became an excuse for drunken and disorderly behaviour. Eventually, a vicar locked the church door against the mourners and removed the rambler rose from the grave. The enraged gypsy queen cursed anyone daring to lock the door in the future. A man who defied her and another who locked the door inadvertently died within the year. The key soon disappeared.

Near the end of the 20th century, the Bishop of Ramsbury was keen to show that the Church wasn't afraid of a gypsy's curse, so Odstock witnessed the bizarre spectacle of clergy descending upon its

St Mary's Church, Odstock

church in order to lock the door! Holy places must be protected from desecration, but should the doors of churches be locked in this manner? Is the emphasis being placed on the worship of property, whether it be a church building, the valuables within it, or a horse, rather than seeking the spirit that led to Joshua Scamp's self-sacrifice?

The major ley or spirit path that runs south from Stonehenge (Walk 19) through Old Sarum to Salisbury Cathedral (Walk 23) continues to Clearbury Ring. This alignment extends southwards to Frankenbury Camp (see Walk 18 in *Walks in Mysterious Hampshire*, in this series by the same author and publisher) and reaches the sea at Highcliffe Castle.

The Walk

1. Go east to pass the letterbox on your left. Pass The Avenue on your right (you will return down this) and come to St Mary's Church on your right. Continue towards Nunton.

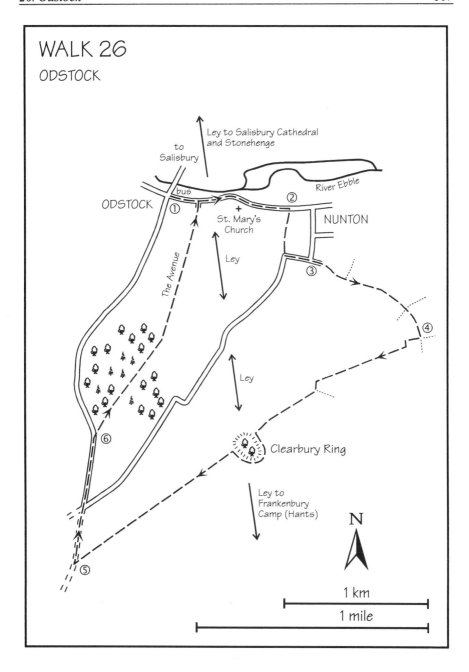

WALK 26
ODSTOCK

Ley to Salisbury Cathedral and Stonehenge

to Salisbury

bus

ODSTOCK

① St. Mary's Church

② River Ebble

NUNTON

③

④

The Avenue

Ley

Ley

⑥

Clearbury Ring

Ley to Frankenbury Camp (Hants)

⑤

N

1 km

1 mile

2. Turn right up a track opposite Nunton Farm. This is Nunton Drove. Pass farm buildings on your left. Turn left at a road.

3. When the road bends left, take a track straight ahead to gradually bear right uphill. Ignore a waymarked footpath on your left and ignore a private road on your left. Pass a bridleway on your left and take a waymarked footpath over a stile ahead to continue beside a hedge on your right. Cross a stile into the next field.

4. Turn right along the right-hand edge of a field, climbing uphill. At the top, go left as waymarked for 30 metres, then bear right along a track beside a hedge on your right to reach Clearbury Ring. Go left around this Iron Age hill fort, now clothed by trees. Continue over a stile beside a gate and descend with a hedge on your right. Keep it there as you proceed through two more sets of gates to reach a track.

5. Turn right down a broad, hedged track. Go ahead at a crossroads.

6. Bear right when the road goes left, leaving you to take a track past woodland. Emerge through a gate out of the wood and follow a tree-lined avenue. Take a gate ahead to continue along the right-hand edge of a field, then past farm buildings on your right to reach the road. Here you go left to retrace your steps to the crossroads and bus stop.

27. THE PEPPERBOX

Route: Pepperbox Hill – Grimstead Beeches – Whiteparish

Distance: 3½ miles. Easy. Linear route with bus stops at both ends.

Maps: OS Pathfinder 1263 Romsey, OS Landranger 184 Salisbury.

Start: Pepperbox Hill (SU210248).

Finish: Whiteparish (SU242235).

Access: Both ends of this route are linked by buses X7 (Salisbury to Southampton) and 34 (Salisbury to Romsey). Telephone 0345 090899 for details.

A Curious Folly

Enjoy panoramic views from the ridgeway and delight in the wild flowers, birds and butterflies on the natural chalk downland owned by the National Trust. The Pepperbox remains a mystery. Known

The Pepperbox

Eyre's Folly, it was built of brick as long ago as 1606. Octagonal in shape, its roof is a pyramid-shape. Mundane explanations are that Gyles Eyre built the tower in order to look down on his neighbours, with their high towers at Longford Castle, and that it was erected to allow ladies to watch falconry and hunting from its upper storey. I can report that I found six leys converging on it, using my dowsing rods, so Mr Eyre may have been privy to some arcane knowledge. Suggest that somebody erected a monument where leys meet and that you have dowsed the said leys exposes you to easy ridicule from cynics, however. They can't argue with the fact that the Pepperbox exists, so that can't be dismissed! Ponder here yet another of Wiltshire's mysteries.

The Walk

1. Go east along the signposted track for the Pepperbox (National Trust). Pass the folly on your right and enjoy the view over the vale on your left. Continue through the woodland of Grimstead Beeches.

2. Fork right on the higher track.

3. Turn right at a crosstracks to descend through downland and pass two patches of trees on your right.

4. Go ahead along a waymarked woodland path. Continue along a hedged track down to Whiteparish, where you go right to the bus stops.

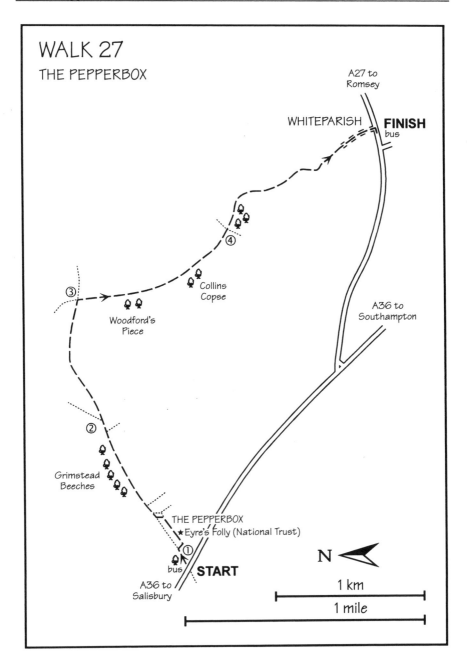

WALK 27
THE PEPPERBOX

A27 to
Romsey

WHITEPARISH
bus
FINISH

A36 to
Southampton

③

Collins
Copse

④

Woodford's
Piece

②

Grimstead
Beeches

THE PEPPERBOX
★ Eyre's Folly (National Trust)

①

bus

START

A36 to
Salisbury

N

1 km

1 mile

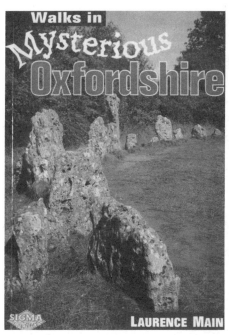

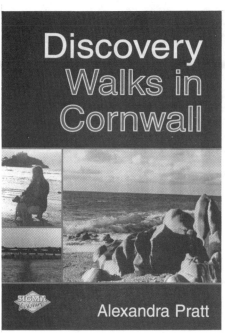

DISCOVERY WALKS IN CORNWALL

Alexandra Pratt

This new book follows less frequented paths to Cornwall's secret places. From mysterious stone circles to lost villages and Dark Age castles, Alexandra offers visitors and residents some of the best walking in this beautiful and magical land. All walks are circular, accompanied by sketch maps and photographs, and are clearly delineated with detailed instructions. £6.95

TEA SHOP WALKS IN SOMERSET

Elizabeth Fowler

These walks are all circular, from 2 to 9 miles and are accompanied by explanatory text on the half hidden pearls of interest to be found along the way. To complete the experience you are invited to visit the tea rooms in the towns and villages featured on the routes, each an excellent quality (and well-deserved!) refreshment break. £6.95

TEA SHOP WALKS IN NORTH DEVON

Norman & June Buckley

Nothing could be more enjoyable than a walk with a welcoming tea shop - and where else can this be better realised than in North Devon, land of fine coastal scenery and the world-famed cream tea? The walks - mainly gentle rambles between two and seven miles - take you along lanes and established footpaths accompanied by clear descriptions, sketch maps, notes on local history and landscape, and the authors' own stunning photographs. A must for locals and visitors to the area. £6.95

TEA SHOP WALKS IN SOUTH DEVON AND DARTMOOR

Norman & June Buckley

Follow these routes and sample the most classic of tea shop walking experiences. Where else better than in South Devon, land of fine coastal scenery, glorious Dartmoor, and above all, the world-famed Devonshire cream tea?' £6.95

BEST PUB WALKS IN THE COTSWOLDS

Laurence Main

The Cotswolds provide many excellent walking opportunities, plus the chance to discover its unique and characterful pubs. Let Laurence show you around! *£6.95*

BEST PUB WALKS IN CORNWALL

Laurence Main

Both coastal and countryside walks are to be found in this excellent book, with a Real Ale pub in every village to be visited. £6.95

BEST PUB WALKS IN NORTH DEVON

Dennis Needham

Devon is a tourist paradise, yet few get off the beaten track to explore the delights of country walking and the wealth of tiny Devonshire pubs. Be one of the few! £6.95

PUB WALKS IN SOUTH DEVON

Laurence Main

Laurence, with his interest in Earth mysteries and ghostly goings-on, shows that there are all sorts of spirits to be found in Devon - and only some of them in the local hostelries. £6.95

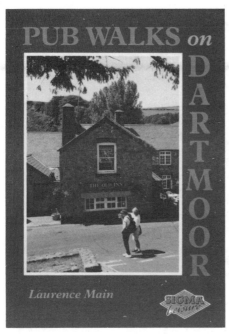